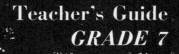

Teacher's Guide
GRADE 7

*i believe
in*

GOD
THE
FATHER

by *William M. Horn*

edited by *Frank W. Klos*

illustrated by *Rey Abruzzi*

LUTHERAN CHURCH PRESS, PHILADELPHIA

LCA WEEKDAY CHURCH SCHOOL SERIES

9936-A64   Printed in U.S.A.   LB333

INTRODUCTION

This course is one of eleven in the "LCA Weekday Church School Series." It is the first of three courses designed specifically for catechetical instruction. Under the closely graded plan of the weekday school this course will be used in grade seven.

Using the general theme "I Believe and I Respond," the three catechetical courses explore the teachings of Luther's *Small Catechism* and relate them to the structure of the Apostles' Creed. While all the elements of the *Small Catechism* will be given consideration in each year, certain parts will receive greater attention. Grade seven focuses on the First Article of the Creed in the first term and on the Lord's Prayer in the second term.

The objective for the first term is to help the young person develop a more mature understanding of and warmer relationship with God the Father, particularly as he has revealed himself through his son.

In the second term, the objective is to help the young person develop a more mature understanding of worship and prayer, particularly the Lord's Prayer and to help him form regular habits of prayer and worship.

The following pages provide teaching helps for both units and sessions and include activity suggestions and resource material for class discussion.

The Editor

Page

Introduction 3

Section One: Preparing to
    Teach the Course 6
The Pupils You Teach 6
The Local Picture 9
The Unit Plan 9
The Three Years' Catechetical
    Program 16
Person-to-Person Teaching 17

Section Two: Theological
    Background Articles 20
God the Father and Creator
    by Martin J. Heinecken 20
Prayer and the Lord's Prayer
    by Edgar M. Carlson 30

Section Three: Teaching Plans
    for Term 1 42
Unit A. Introduction to
             Confirmation 42
Unit B. Beliefs That Matter 62
Unit C. God as Father 76

Section Four: Teaching Plans
    for Term 2 100
Unit D. Prayer 100
Unit E. The Lord's Prayer 113
Unit F. Public Worship 143
Unit G. The Service 156

CONTENTS

SECTION 1

SECTION ONE

preparing to teach the course

Good, effective teaching depends upon adequate preparation. The more time you spend getting ready to teach, the more satisfactory your teaching experiences will be and—what is even more important—the more you will be able to help your pupils learn.

You need to know your pupils both as a group of seventh-graders and as individuals. You need to be aware of their interests and concerns, of how they learn, and of the teaching methods and procedures to which they respond.

Two background articles by prominent theologians are included in this book. One article discusses the First Article of the Apostles' Creed and the other explores the significance of the Lord's Prayer. These readings are for your personal growth in understanding the parts of Luther's *Small Catechism* which you will be teaching. As you immerse yourself in the subject matter of this course you will have little difficulty in guiding your pupils from the rich resources of your own personal religious experiences.

THE PUPILS YOU TEACH

No pupil can show such a variety of characteristics as the early adolescent. In many ways he defies classification, being a colt on one occasion, a mule on another. Twelve-year-olds run the gamut from childishness and giggling to strong loyalties and penetrating questions. They can fluctuate from one extreme to another for no apparent reason.

Mentally your pupils are entering the stage where they reason things out, probe old truths with new questions, raise doubts about what before was accepted without a whimper. They ask, How come? Who says so? What authority has he for saying so? (You will find the pupil's book for this year cast in this vein, as though pupils were challenging long-held ideas, searching for an authority, looking for answers of their own.)

Socially they are more and more drawn to those their own age, talking alike, thinking alike, acting alike. The group itself becomes a mighty force in teaching. You will do well to discover the natural leaders of your group, win their confidence, and appeal to their leadership in carrying out group plans.

Enthusiasm is a mark of this age—enthusiasm for whatever captures and holds their interest, be it sports, books, science, or exploration.

6

If the twelve-year-old is brought in on group plans, on research areas, on choosing assignments, he will enter in beyond the call of duty.

Some rather obvious points should be kept in mind in dealing with these pupils:

1. Treat each pupil as a person in his own right; respect his judgment and point of view, however faulty they may seem.

2. Tailor your teaching to the individual pupil, much as a dressmaker tailors a pattern to the particular individual who is to wear the dress. You will need to get to know each pupil personally in order to do this.

3. Enlist each pupil's co-operation by bringing him into group planning and letting him volunteer for various assignments.

4. Capitalize on each pupil's special interest or talent. Even the slow or withdrawn pupil can take a respected part in group plans.

Take as little advantage as possible of outside pressures to motivate the pupil to participate in confirmation instruction. Such devices as report cards or periodic appeals to parents should be used sparingly.

A gathering of parents and pupils at the opening of the first term should be sufficient to apprise both groups of what is expected over the three-year course and to indicate the specific emphases of this course. Similar meetings can be held at the beginning of the second and third years of catechetical training.

Four Basic Pointers in Teaching

Whether you teach seventh-graders or first-graders, certain basic considerations lie behind your teaching. If you take stock of them from time to time, they will help in your approach, attitude, and guidance of pupils. These considerations are:

1. Nothing is really taught unless it is learned. The objectives for this course are stated in terms of pupils' learning, not of content coverage. What happens to and within the pupil—not merely in amassing information, but in changing attitudes and goals and patterns of action—is paramount. This makes your task the more difficult to measure. You can easily determine his mastery of knowledge; but how do you test changes in attitudes or goals or patterns of action? Whether measurable or not, your objectives will be directed toward his learning.

2. Keep in mind how you learned. You doubtless learn more by teaching than by sitting as a pupil. When you teach, you have a special motivation for learning. Your Bible study suddenly gets a special point; so does your review of the Christian faith; so does your probing of pertinent issues. How can this incentive be transferred to a pupil? Remember that learning takes place when it *serves a purpose for the learner.* Strive to awaken pupils' readiness to learn by helping them realize that the desired learnings of the course really meet their needs and interests. If the suggestions offered in the sessions here don't strike you as incentive enough, plan some of your own.

3. Your pupils represent widely different backgrounds. How much do you know of a pupil's family life? His past record of Christian training? The attitude of his home toward confirmation and participation in the life of the church? What about his individual traits: outgoing or withdrawn? natural leader or follower? What about his personal friendships? From which schools does he come? Is his only attachment to the class group that of the church itself, and not the neighborhood or school or club? What is his range of special interests, his hobbies, his leisure time pursuits?

Home visits are important here where few facts are known. The pastor could probably provide considerable information. Previous church school teachers might help too, though some pupils get "labeled" through judgments of teachers. The guidance counselor at the junior high school may be of valuable assistance.

Occasional visits to church activities that involve seventh-graders (Intermediate Luther League, scouts, or social programs) are especially helpful; here you see the pupil with others his own age. Such visits should be by way of listening posts—not spying or trying to be one of the gang.

While your concern is for a whole group, don't lose sight of individuals within it. Each pupil listens to you with one single set of ears and watches with one set of eyes. While your "you" will at times be plural, a pupil finds it more meaningful when the "you" is singular.

4. Don't underestimate the teaching value of your own attitude and the class atmosphere.

Your enthusiasm for a subject is bound to be catching. Your experience as a "big brother" or seasoned Christian veteran counts for much, whether you have all the answers or not. Part of your teaching, especially in dealing with matters of Christian faith and Christian life, will be personal testimony—stating what you believe, why you believe it—whether it rests on solid grounds or not. Let the pupil know that you are a fellow learner.

Attitudes teach in indirect ways. In the carefulness of your preparation and the regularity of your attendance the pupil reads something of his importance in your eyes. He figures he doesn't count for much if you give the class session low priority in time, thought, or concern.

A relaxed atmosphere, an enthusiasm for the work at hand, a feeling of its importance, an expectation of the best from pupils— these should reduce discipline problems to a minimum. However, temptations to "cut up" may be avoided by such provisions as spaced seating arrangement, privacy of surroundings, having materials at hand in advance, and devising certain "rules of order."

THE LOCAL PICTURE

Conditions in your particular congregation will have a bearing on your plans for this course. In consultation with the committee on Christian education of your church, give consideration to the following:

1. What will be the size of the class? In this course a maximum of 15 pupils should be set. Even though your enrollment for the course may reach 40 or 50, remember that it is far better to subdivide a large group into smaller classes than to inhibit learning by overcrowded conditions. If multiple classes are necessary, scheduling should be done according to a wise use of facilities and teachers.

2. What about grading? Confirmation instruction usually enrolls all twelve-year-olds, including young people who have never attended Sunday church school and children of prospective church members. Are they to be placed in the same group as those with considerable background and training? What about twelve-year-olds who are in special schools or special grades? Will their age or grade in school be the common denominator? Generally, the Long-Range Program suggests grouping according to public school grade. This class then would be composed of seventh-graders, although special consideration should be given to "special" pupils.

3. What rapport with the home is expected? Does your church lean heavily on home support for homework assignments and faithfulness in attendance? Plan at least one parent-leader meeting at the beginning of the course to discuss the course's scope and desirable parent co-operation.

4. What administrative details should be considered? The renting of films or filmstrips; room facilities with blackboard; audio-visual equipment, with guidance or personnel for its operation; materials at class disposal (such as paper, pencils, and tables or writing surfaces); resource books for the teacher's use—all must be planned for. While these concerns may seem minor, adequate preparation can prevent many sources of irritation once the course has begun.

THE UNIT PLAN

Teachers unfamiliar with the unit plan may at first be confused by the time schedule expected and find it hard to chart progress. However, if you have ever tried to compress a large amount of material into limited time, or if you have found yourself running dry with large amounts of time still to be used, you'll quickly welcome the unit plan for teaching.

Session-by-session suggestions are offered in this teaching guide to give your teaching plans a start. The session guidance shows you workable ways of dividing up the unit time. Modify these session plans or substitute session plans of your own. Do what you think is best to help your pupils accomplish the unit objectives in the time available. The only time limits set are for the units themselves. Thus, you can carry over unfinished work to the next session, or set your own pace when suggestions given here seem too skimpy for a whole session.

Various factors will affect your teaching speed: the interest of your pupils; the rapidity of their learning; the importance you or they may attach to certain issues or teachings. Discussion questions are always an unknown quantity, when it comes to allotting time. The same question that provokes a half-hour exploration in one class may misfire with another.

Number of Sessions

Before beginning the course, chart the number of sessions your class will have during the year. The school calendar will be of help on this, especially if you customarily suspend weekday school classes when the public school is not in session or when holiday seasons come.

Your year may run anywhere from 28 to 34 sessions; the structure of this course makes allowance for such a range. But it's important at the outset to plan where to compress and where to expand, because the closing sessions involve some basic studies, and you won't want to have to skip them for lack of time.

Basically, the course has thirty sessions (corresponding to the chapters in the pupil's book). However, each term provides two additional sessions for use as needed. In the first term, for example, the first two units allow for an extra session each. These should be used only if your year runs beyond the average of thirty sessions.

Change of Pace

The general plan calls for sessions of sixty minutes. While the seventh-grader has a rather long interest span, he seldom maintains interest in one thing for a whole hour. You will need frequent change of pace.

Suggestions in the session plans offer a variety of learning experiences—from leader-controlled discussions, to Bible explorations, to research projects, to pupil-led activities. You must be the best judge of transitions, moving from one type of learning experience to another before pupil interest drops too sharply. In general, the session suggestions call for discussion and mental work earlier in the period, when pupils may be expected to be fairly alert, and for activities and research projects toward the latter part of the session. However, do not follow the same routine every week. A sameness of pattern soon becomes dull.

10

A Warning

These sessions are going to make you stop and think. If you don't find yourself puzzled at times, they won't have succeeded. They are meant to lead pupils to think, to become curious, to ask questions—as well as to suggest lines along which answers are to be sought. You may find them opening up areas of exploration that you yourself have not plumbed. An underlying purpose here is to move pupils to ask questions.

Your role is seen as fellow-learner, a bit more seasoned, a bit abler to put things into their proper place, but still a fellow-learner. This is no spot for a walking encyclopedia on religion and the teaching guide is no answer book.

This makes your task more difficult, but more exciting. Convince your pupils that you are a fellow-learner. That puts your approach on a "let's-do-this-thing-together" basis.

Worship

Your class probably will meet—separately or with other classes of seventh-graders—for a brief period of class worship. Pupils themselves can conduct this worship. You may wish to follow some pattern of alphabetical rotation in the leadership from week to week; or you may ask for volunteers; or you may restrict the leadership to the more capable pupils. An ability to read well will be a necessary criterion in selecting leaders. Bungled reading may help the reader, but it scarcely edifies a group.

Ten minutes will provide enough time for worship. Scripture reading, prayer, and the Lord's Prayer will be kept at a minimum. Scripture passages can be chosen normally from "To Read and Think About" sections given in most chapters of the pupil's book. (The chapter numbers in the pupil's book correspond to the session numbers given here.) Encourage pupils to prepare their own prayers, however brief. Introduce them to the great prayers of the church in either collect form or hymn form.

In the first term the use of Luther's explanation of the First Article of the Creed also should be used weekly as an act of worship. It is an excellent affirmation of faith. Its weekly use will not only give sharpness to expressions of faith in worship, but also aid in the pupils' memorization. Pupils may read it together from the *Small Catechism* printed in their pupil's book. Encourage them, as time goes on, to rely less and less on reading.

The occasional use of hymns, whether sung or read, also will be appropriate. Twelve-year-olds, especially boys with voices beginning to change, shy away from singing. Therefore, unless you have a capable pianist in the group (and a piano), hymns should be read.

At first pupils will need guidance in worship. If you have modern translations of the Bible available, they might be put at the pupils' disposal for Scripture readings. (This is especially helpful if pupils use a different translation for study in the class session or home reading.) Assistance in phrasing prayers also may be needed.

Since the second term deals with worship and prayer, such things as sentence prayers, prayer hymns, and frequent repetition of classic collects should come more into play. Luther's explanations of the various parts of the Lord's Prayer may be used also. If the "affirmation of faith" has proved effective in the first term, you may suggest that each of Luther's meanings be prefaced by "I believe that. . . ." (Try it, using the meaning of the First Petition as an example.)

Worship is viewed here as worship for its own sake, not primarily as a teaching device, nor as a training for leadership. It is meant to set the atmosphere for the whole session. Have all plans carefully made before the class session to avoid a last-minute scurrying about. Plan for variety in the worship experiences. Don't get into a rut.

Bible Study

Bible passages are suggested in the pupil's book in groups of seven (one for each day of the week). Each group is a selection of passages relevant to its chapter in the pupil's book. The passages, as well as being worship materials, provide readings for the pupil's daily devotions and offer scriptural resources for closer scrutiny in the class session.

How faithfully pupils will follow these readings in private devotions is largely up to them. No check-up device is suggested to see if they keep up (though you will discover this in their class response). In outlining the course procedure at the outset, you may appeal to pupils to make a habit of daily Bible reading and prayer. Help them feel an identification with the whole group in this—a feeling that each pupil is reading the same passage the same day, weaving a bond within the group. Let each decide the time of day when he will make this a regular practice. Help them feel they are keeping a solemn covenant with each other. Suggest that they attempt to let the passage evoke the prayer, even though they don't always find words coming. Give them some rule of thumb for reading, like asking themselves, "What does this passage have to do with me?" Encourage them to underline verses or phrases that strike fire for them.

Since Bible study is made a part of every class session, considerable ingenuity should be brought to bear to avoid monotony. For many sessions you may prepare a list of questions that will give special significance to the study. If, for example, the golden rule is the verse for study, you may ask about its application. How literally are we to take these words? Do we render tit for tat, saluting those who salute us, inviting those who may return the invitation? Who takes the initiative here? What should be the motive? Can this rule be used selfishly? (When space permits, such pointers are given in the session plans.)

In most instances you will view the passage against its relevance to discussion issues or points raised in the session. In virtually every study, therefore, you'll ask what light the passage throws on the question at hand.

While the Revised Standard Version will be used throughout the course, other translations can be of help to pupils, especially as they help illuminate the more difficult passages. In such instances you might ask what fresh insights a different translation gives.

Whenever passages from the four Gospels occur, reference can be made to Sunday church school studies. On Sundays seventh-graders are studying the life of Jesus; cognizance is taken of this in selecting passages. Many passages will reinforce what has already been taught in the Sunday church school; others will set familiar passages against different issues, causing new facets to become visible.

Since some pupils will have little familiarity with the Bible, you should be alert to the problem of developing their skill in locating passages without consulting the table of contents. An occasional five- or ten-minute speed drill might serve this purpose (and also provide the session with a change of pace). Type several references (John 3:16, Exodus 20:7) on sheets of paper; give each pupil one list of references and a pair of scissors; set a stop watch; and see how long it takes to find all references, cutting the Bible reference from the paper and using the slips as bookmarks as passages are located. If you want pupils to do the work together, see how many references they can find in a specified time.

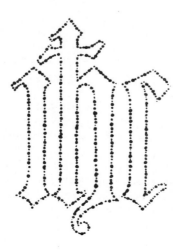

Homework and Assignments

Except for research projects, the class sessions will not depend on assignments carried out by pupils between class sessions. This does not mean that homework is not expected. Pupils will be expected to read their book. It is designed for a several-sitting reading (perhaps by units); but it can also be assigned on a session-to-session basis. Pupils should be encouraged to read it through early in the course, then to review specific chapters as homework preparation for following sessions. By averting reading in class, you allow more class time for picking out salient points and sharpening issues for discussion.

All in all, the pupil's book is intended to whet the appetite for discussing points and issues in the class session. The more familiar pupils are with the book's contents through pre-session reading, the more productive discussions will be.

The same principle holds for Bible passages. If pupils have used the appointed readings in private devotions, they will need little review in the class session. However, you should not assume this familiarity on the part of all pupils; a class reading of passages, then, may be expected in the Bible study.

Session plans indicate which research projects are suitable for extra-session exploration and which are intended for group use in the session itself. Dates when reports are due should be clearly stated when reports are assigned. Remember to allot time for hearing reports when they are due. Nothing encourages dilatory attention to assignments so much as delays or forgetfulness in asking for reports.

Since this is the first of three pre-confirmation courses, you may expect certain out-of-session requirements of pupils. Attendance at public worship should certainly be one. In some churches reports of sermons are asked of each pupil (a matter that needs some guidance from the pastor). Pupils may be expected to sit together for church service or with their families. Whatever the mode of participation in the ongoing life of the church, determine in advance what is expected and make it clear to pupils at the outset. And even if custom does not dictate such assignments, you might initiate them for your own pupils.

Place of Catechism in the Course

Luther's *Small Catechism* is printed at the end of the pupil's book. It is basic to the three-year confirmation instruction.

The parts of the Catechism are always set in a larger context. The First Article is viewed against the broader sphere of faith and belief, the Lord's Prayer against the larger backdrop of worship and the life of prayer. The implications of various parts of the Catechism thus provide the wider sphere within which the parts are studied. Thus, the Catechism is not studied per se or as a little book of Christian truth—rather, as a

14

tool, in somewhat the fashion as the Bible itself is viewed here as a tool.

Your objective is in terms of the pupil's commitment of his life to Christ. The Catechism plays its role through compressing the truths of the Christian faith and life into brief form. This does not underplay the importance of the Catechism; it merely takes your teaching beyond the mental mastery of catechetical words.

Memorization

Throughout the entire three years, the memorizing of parts of the *Small Catechism* will be expected. You may have to adjust the requirements for memorizing to a pupil's capacity in special cases. (An occasional pupil is mentally incapable of memorizing more than the bare essentials of the Ten Commandments, Lord's Prayer, or Apostles' Creed.) Remember that confirmation depends far more on attitudes than mental acumen.

Seek devices that will reduce sheer rote memorizing to a minimum. Suggestions offered under "Worship" above provide one such device. (How did *you* learn the Lord's Prayer by heart? By sheer will power and deliberate assault? Or by repeated use without any intention of memorizing?) No special harm is done when the whole group repeats sections of the Catechism by heart, with the laggard carried along for the time being. The underlining of key words in a section (like the three *p*'s— preserves, provides, protects—in Luther's explanation of the First Article) can also aid pupils.

The fixed portions of The Service, a selection of great hymns, and some classic collects are among other materials suitable for memorization. Pupils' frequent use of them in class worship will aid in memorizing, as will pupils' participation in public worship (ask them to see how little they must use their hymnals as the year progresses). Use the principle of frequent exposure rather than any direct insistence on rote memorizing. No attempts should be made to check up on individual pupils here.

Teaching Tools

Unit introductions will provide you with lists of materials needed for class sessions. Before each unit begins assemble materials needed for the entire unit, especially those involving research projects and lengthy assignments.

If classroom space is large enough, some resources can be laid out on a table for browsing or class use. Aids in Bible study will be especially useful here: concordances, Bible dictionaries, Bible commentaries, various translations of the Bible. Books of prayers and hymnals should be standard equipment for assistance in worship. Arrangements may be made with the pastor and church library for borrowing books and pamphlets that bear upon various unit themes. In some units you may want to arrange a display (for instance, of various hymnals used by your church at different periods or publications from various epochs in the history of your church).

Certain aids will prove helpful for your own preparation. The *Book of Concord* incorporates the *Large Catechism*, an expansion of the *Small Catechism*. Your publishing house issues books and booklets dealing with such subjects as: teaching Luther's Catechism, explaining The Service, meditations on and studies of the Lord's Prayer and Apostles' Creed, examining the life of worship and prayer. Your pastor will prove helpful both in lending and recommending books along this line.

THE THREE-YEAR CATECHETICAL PROGRAM

This is the first of three years of catechetical instruction. All three are based on the *Small Catechism*. The plan suggests that pupils be confirmed at the end of the ninth grade or at fourteen years of age.

Each year certain elements of the Catechism will be given major treatment in depth while other elements are covered more rapidly. In this seventh grade, the First Article of the Creed and Lord's Prayer are studied; in the eighth grade, the Second Article and the Ten Commandments; in the ninth grade, the Third Article and the sacraments.

Note the main themes of later catechetical courses—not that you will thereby avoid transgressing, but that you may tailor your emphases in this course accordingly. While you can't avoid stressing stewardship in dealing with the First Article of the Creed, it does become a major emphasis later on. The same will be true of church history, of the Christian view of man and sin, and of the church. In many cases you will be laying a groundwork for these later emphases. Your major attention in the first term here will be to faith, on God as Father; in the second term, to prayer and worship. Within the span of this seventh-grade course you'll frequently find a repetition of themes (as in the case of worship, where in Unit A you deal with it in a minor way and in the second term study it in greater detail). Your anticipating occasions for laying groundwork and your reinforcing previous learning will make your teaching more effective.

Each of the three catechetical courses has a definite structure. The first term emphasizes matters of faith under the heading "I Believe"; the second term emphasizes matters of life under the heading "I Respond." Put differently, the course sets God's confrontation of us against our response. He confronts me as Father Creator; I respond in worship and prayer. He confronts me as Lord and Savior; I respond in a life which uses the Ten Commandments as a guide. (Of course this doesn't mean that you reserve the "response" for the second term. Whenever God confronts us there is some kind of response—more an interchange, such as we find in public worship.)

16

Since catechetical instruction has usually been the responsibility of the pastor, it is expected that he will teach the ninth-grade courses and perhaps the eighth-grade course as well. The seventh-grade course is designed for lay teaching, though the pastor may be asked to conduct the opening unit of four or five sessions. (If he can conduct the entire course, he may do so, using the suggestions here and expanding them as he sees fit.)

The time schedule may pose some problems, if the pastor is to lead in the opening unit and if this class meets at the same hour as one of the other two catechetical classes. You may wish to schedule the opening of the course some four to five weeks ahead of the eighth- and ninth-grade classes, or adjust it by some other plan to the pastor's schedule. You also may wish to combine several seventh-grade classes into one large group for the opening unit.

In any event—whether the pastor does or does not conduct this opening unit—you as a lay teacher should be part of the class session, if for no other reason than to sit in and get better acquainted with the pupils.

PERSON-TO-PERSON TEACHING

Your role in teaching is essentially a person-to-person role. Few persons can remember precepts given them by their teachers. It's possible that you can't remember a single statement any one of your own teachers ever made (and if you do remember, chances are that it isn't one you were meant to remember). But you do remember the impact of their personalities. Even more, you remember the accumulation of learning experiences.

This is in a measure a comfort to all who teach. You can make mistakes, but you remember them better than your pupils will. You can misfire in an occasional session, but there's always a next session. You can feel frustrated if pupils are slow to learn and show little measurable progress. Yet something happens. The Holy Spirit works wonders through us even though we are at times disciples of clay, weak vessels used as instruments of his power. His stake in this venture is far greater than yours; so, while much seems to depend on you, you can leave the end results up to him.

SECTION 2

SECTION TWO

Theological Background Articles

God the Father and Creator

*An examination of the First Article
of the Apostles' Creed*

By Martin J. Heinecken

It is important to stress how the Creed's expression of faith in Father, Son, and Holy Ghost came into being. We say that our God is one God but that there are three persons in the Godhead. We thus refer to God as the Trinity. However, there is no doctrine of the Trinity taught in the Bible. As a matter of fact no formal doctrines as such are taught in the Bible. It simply witnesses to God's deeds and interprets them. The Bible describes God in his personal dealings with men which require their personal response of obedience-in-trust. The church's doctrines (teachings) developed for teaching purposes, to organize its teachings consistently, and to safeguard these teachings against misrepresentations. It is not the acceptance of the church's doctrines that saves a man, but his faith in the God whom the doctrines present.

THE NEW TESTAMENT WITNESS

The first Christians knew, worshiped, and proclaimed only the God whom they had met on life's road in the person of Jesus Christ, by the power of the Holy Spirit. Those who were Jews among them recognized Jesus as the promised Christ (Messiah, Anointed One). They saw in him the same God whom their fathers had worshiped (Matthew 16:16), the same God who had created the world (John 1:1). In fact, the true nature of the God of their fathers became clear to them only in Jesus, the Christ. In him God stood fully revealed as holy love; therefore, in him the Old Testament picture of God, as well as heathen notions of God, were both corrected and fulfilled (John 1:1-4; 14:9-10; 20:28). Equally emphatic is the confession of the disciples that none of this was clear to them except in the power of God himself, present to them in the Holy Spirit (Acts 1, 2; 1 Corinthians 12:2). They recognized that they themselves had been changed and had been given a new life, mind, heart, and tongue. They had been born again, and for such a rebirth the creative Spirit of God himself alone was sufficient (John 3).

THE NATURE OF REVELATION

The doctrine of the Trinity is the direct result of God's revelation of himself to us. God initiates revelation; he chooses himself a people; he speaks through the prophets; he sends the Son. Revelation does not mean that man discovers God by seeking him, but that God comes to man and actively discloses and imparts himself. It is like when marriage partners voluntarily, in love, disclose and give themselves to each other in the most intimate union. (Note the biblical use of the word "know" to designate both the marriage union [Genesis 4:1] and the union of God and man [Amos 3:2].) God himself is present in his revelation (Jesus is called Immanuel, "God with us") and he himself must open our eyes to see that it is he. Through God alone is God known.

THE FOURTH-CENTURY DOCTRINE OF THE TRINITY

In the fourth century, in conflict with heresies, the early Christians spelled out their beliefs in the doctrine of the Trinity. Here the Father, Son, and Holy Ghost are each distinct and yet remain one God. This distinction, reflected in the Apostles' Creed, confesses God the Father as the Creator, God the Son as the Redeemer, and God the Holy Spirit as the Sanctifier (the one who makes us holy). But these are not three Gods. It was stressed that each member of the Trinity was so fully God that there could be no question that the same God who made the world also redeemed it and then founded the church through which men might be re-created and restored to the purpose of their creation. All three works—creation, redemption, and sanctification—are the acts of the same God and are rooted in the very nature of God.

ONE GOD OF HOLY LOVE

The unifying nature of God which is characteristic of all his works is holy love. His holiness and his love cannot be separated. His holiness speaks of his wholeness, his purity, his unalterable opposition to sin, his separateness from all his creation. His love, however, always appears in the background of his holiness and speaks of his acts in terms of his concern for his beloved. This love, therefore, is quite different from what men commonly regard as love. The Greek word *agape* best describes this totally outgiving love of God. Unfortunately, there is no good English equivalent for *agape*. We must still use the word love, but with this sense of *agape*. God's love, then, is spontaneous, unselfish, and free. It is unlimited, unconditional. His love leads to the creation of men; this love gives men their worth. It is best characterized as love for the enemy, a love directed toward those who do not love in return but who actually hate. This love is not to be confused with mere "liking." "Liking" has its proper place in life, but must be clearly distinguished from "love" (Luke 15:2; Romans 5:8).

Every statement about God is, therefore, a statement about this God of love, even when it refers to his wrath and judgment. It is the God of love who is all-wise, all-powerful, all-seeing, faithful, wrathful, and so on. God made the world out of love for no other reason but that he might shed his love upon it.

CREATION, REDEMPTION, AND SANCTIFICATION DISTINGUISHED

While all God's works are performed by the same God of love, they are not the same and are not to be confused. God's work of creation, although it is a work of love, is not redemptive. You cannot be saved from sin and death and all the powers of evil in the world just by receiving gifts of creation from God. Our wonderful bodies, our powers of mind, all the marvelous treasures of the earth bless us without our deserving (Matthew 5:45). They do, but how we misuse them! Thus they cannot redeem us from sin.

Only God himself can rescue us from our lost condition. He does this through the work of redemption, an act of recovering for us what we have lost. Redemption is a struggle and a victory over evil powers; it is an act of vicarious suffering and atonement. Christ is not a second God, a more loving person who saves us from the sternness of the Father's judgment. It is the same God the Father, who in Christ reconciles the world unto himself (2 Corinthians 5:19).

God saves men in history, where their fall from his grace has taken place. For this act God became incarnate; he became man in history. He lived and suffered, was crucified, and rose again from the dead that all men might believe in his love and be saved (John 3:16-17). The good news of that once-and-for-all event of what God did for men through Christ is called the gospel.

Then there follows the work of sanctification, of making the sinner into a saint. Here God gives his own life-giving power to men through the Holy Spirit to help them become the kind of people he intends them to be. Through Christ God's work of redemption was done once and for all, but through the Holy Spirit and the work of sanctification God continually renews and restores his people. Thus Jesus had to die on the cross, be resurrected, and ascend to the right hand of power before the Holy Spirit could come and the church be formed. And so, it is helpful to distinguish God's works of creation, redemption, and sanctification as long as we do not parcel out these works to three separate divine beings.

THE DANGER OF A ONE-SIDED GOD

In trying to understand the magnitude of God there is another danger. That is, we may reduce him to a one-sided being. For instance, one can so emphasize the Fatherhood of God, the goodness of creation, and the common brotherhood of all men that there is no awareness of God, the Redeemer. Then Jesus serves only as an example of a good man whose faith and virtue are to be imitated.

Or the Savior can be overemphasized in a sentimental Jesus-ology with the result that the goodness of creation and the manifestation of God's love in it completely disappear. This distorted Jesus-relation can easily become a private affair in which fellowship with others in the church and the renewing work of the Holy Spirit play no significant role.

Or the indwelling Holy Spirit can be overemphasized, developing an intense religiosity which ignores the stability of the relationship with the Creator Father and his redemptive love in Christ. Mere high-powered enthusiasm is not enough. Speaking with impassioned tongues and shaking and quaking are not guarantees of the new life of God. Every harebrained scheme pulled out of the blue is not Spirit-inspired.

The three articles of the Apostles' Creed help us keep our understanding of God in proper perspective with all his glory and power and love completely unified.

FAITH IN GOD, THE CREATOR

In his explanation of the First Article of the Apostles' Creed Luther makes clear that confession of faith is entirely a matter of personal relationship between man and God. The believer acknowledges his dependence upon a loving Father for everything he is and has. From his personal center he further acknowledges that all other creatures, in fact, the whole universe, depend upon the Creator in the same way. To say that God is the Maker of heaven and earth is not to refer only to the past, but also to recognize and accept a present relationship of absolute dependence upon a loving God.

Merely acknowledging with the mind that some wise and mighty power must have in the distant past made the world is not having faith in God, the Father. Such an acknowledgment is perfectly compatible with the idea of a clock-maker God, who once made the world and keeps it running but has no further dealings with it. (This belief is called "deism.") A man can assert belief in a deistic God without feeling either grateful or obedient. Faith requires worship and a commitment to active obedience.

With a sense of wonder and awe and indebtedness the believer regards his body and all his endowments, together with all the created world, as God's gracious gifts. He doesn't confuse the giver with the gift. He knows that he holds all of God's gifts in trust. This leads to a real sense of stewardship.

The one who does not make this kind of grateful acknowledgment is "offended" by the claim God puts upon him. Why should he be grateful when he has worked hard for what he has? Why should he be grateful when he has so little and others have so much? Why should he acknowledge dependence upon something other than the world he lives in when he depends upon that world for his sustenance?

God asks our daily self-surrender and the right kind of humility regarding our place in creation. Self-surrender is not something that a person can do once and for all. The attitude of praise, thanks, and obedience toward God which Luther described can be maintained only through a daily renewal and a daily overcoming of the temptation of self-sufficiency, pride, ingratitude, and improper stewardship.

DEPENDENCE ON GOD

The Bible constantly witnesses to man's dependence upon God for all of life. This is where the emphasis should fall in the twentieth century. At a time when man is increasing his power tremendously and advancing into space with no limit in sight, he must acknowledge the absolute dependence of all his power upon the gracious Creator God.

Only God has life in and of himself. All other power, energy, and life is derived. Nothing is independent and self-sustaining without God. God alone is eternal, unchangeable, indestructible, without beginning or end, depending on no one but himself. All else in the whole universe, throughout all the reaches of time and space and even beyond into realms that are not accessible to our senses, depends upon him. As the old spiritual exults, "He's got the whole world in his hands." The Apostles' Creed confesses that he is the Maker of heaven and earth; this is all-inclusive. To this the Nicene Creed adds, "Maker of all things visible and invisible," so that there is no mistaking that inclusiveness.

Children today know something of the tremendous age of the world and of its immense size, each a concept to stagger the imagination. They know that it is composed of limitless quantities of electrochemical energy. The universe is so amazing, the power potential of a single atom so unbelievably fantastic, that some of us often are tempted to identify all of this universe of power with God himself. However, this is precisely the fearful idolatry for which St. Paul rebukes the Romans (Romans 1). Because they confused the Creator and the creature they were abandoned by God to the fearful consequences of the inherent confusion. Of course all energy depends upon God for its being; he is the creative ground of all being. Without his free, creative will everything would sink into nothingness.

CREATION

God's revelation does not give an answer to the question of the *how*, but only the *who* and the *why* of creation. If we are asking about

24

the final origin of all things, the *how* remains a conclusive mystery. If we are asking about *how* things developed from a given material, then man can, on the basis of the evidence, set up his reasonable hypotheses. Revelation, alone, answers the *who* and the *why*. The answer lies simply in God and his creative act of love.

The biblical cosmology (i.e., the simple three-story plan of a universe with a flat earth and a heaven above the intervening curtain of the sky) is not a matter of revelation. The Bible is not a textbook in science. It gives no complete, final information about things which men can discover for themselves. The limitless size of the universe is a matter of human discovery. No matter how far man travels in it, he will never discover God or his abode, for God is not a space-time being. This is in an altogether different dimension from that of man, a concept which is quite comprehensible to people today. No cosmology (picture of the universe) can, therefore, *locate* God in the universe because he is *not a part* of it. Nor is he just a name for the whole business (a view called "pantheism"). He is the one who planned it, devised it, brought it forth, ordered it. Today our concept of the greatness of God should increase in direct proportion to our consciousness of the immensity of the universe over which he is sovereign.

Just as the picture of the universe is not a matter of revelation, neither is the manner in which any particular planetary system came to be in its present form. With so many billions of galaxies in space we obviously cannot be concerned only with the *how* of our own planetary system. All this is a matter for sensible scientific hypothesis. Biblical revelation need not be in conflict with science at all, unless the scientist goes beyond his evidence and makes statements about God, whom he can never discover through his microscopes and telescopes or unless the biblical scholar makes statements about science which he cannot substantiate scientifically. When man uses his Godgiven brain to search out these origins, this, too, must be regarded as a work of God, for all knowledge comes from God. All scientific discoveries which give man greater control over the forces of nature are indeed God's gifts. And God must be thanked for them.

THE GENESIS ACCOUNT

While many persons continue to make a cosmogony (a theory of the creation of the world) of the first chapter of Genesis and seek to harmonize it with scientific views of a gradual, orderly development, this is an abuse of the Bible. The Genesis account can be harmonized with science at best only in a general sort of way. It is clearly not a scientific account in the modern sense of that word.

The revelatory content of Genesis concerns the *who* and *why*. The statements may briefly sum this up: (1) There is one God of love to whose creative will everything owes its being. (2) Creation is an act of God's free decision. It is not a necessity. It is not some kind of spontaneous emanation like the light which flows from the sun. (3) There is an ordered process of development out of a previously created unformed energy. (4) All creatures are made after their king. (5) Man alone is created in God's image. He is the crown of creation. Everything on this earth was made for him, and he was made to glorify God in obedience to his will. (6) The whole creation as it comes from the hand of God is good, and the so-called material cannot, therefore, be the source of evil. The source of evil is not in things, but in the pride and self-will of man who does not use rightly the things God has made. This last point must be strongly emphasized if the right attitude toward the world, toward the body, toward all of life, is to be cultivated. The basic dualism of the Bible is not spiritual (good) versus material (evil), but Creator versus creature.

THE MIRACLE OF THE CREATION OUT OF NOTHING

The concept of a creation out of nothing must be recognized as the basic and absolute miracle underlying everything that is. A miracle is something only God can do. All human "creators" need material out of which to fashion whatever they "create." They cannot, however, "create" the material itself. As far as they are concerned, it is simply there. It was there long before they were and presumably will be there long after they have died.

The material of the universe was certainly not man's creative idea. Man can never, except with what has already been given him, produce energy, just as he cannot produce himself or sustain himself. We can say only that God produced it *out of nothing*. When a magician pulls endless numbers of flags out of nowhere, we know it is all a trick. With time and patience we too could learn the trick. But if the magician produced something out of nothing and could really "materialize" big black Cadillacs complete with chauffeurs at will, we would also worship him. We should understand that God does not produce the world out of himself, like a giant spider spinning its web out of itself. If he did, this would make the world itself a part of God. It is not. Nor does God simply form the world out of a pre-existent chaotic stuff. If he did that stuff would in effect *be* God because God would be dependent upon *it*. This leaves only the genuine miracle of creation—*something out of nothing*.

THE PROBLEM OF THE BEGINNING

We cannot really limit creation to one creative act at one point in time. Creation is continually going on. Every time a child is born, this human center of responsibility is a genuine creation. It comes into being by God's creative act—miraculously, out of nowhere. It did not pre-exist. It does not come from heaven. Though the body is the result of the union of sperm and ovum, the new center of responsibility with a name and an everlasting destiny is God's brand-new creation.

Furthermore, the "something out of nothing" means that God at all times by his creative power sustains the world above the abyss of nothingness into which it would sink if he so chose. It is only by his creative Word that the whole universe continues to be. God actually sustains the order in the universe and is active in its ongoing processes.

If this is our understanding of the Creator, it is pointless to try to date the act of Creation in time, whether you set the date at six thousand or six thousand billion years ago. Space and time are themselves God's creation; God is not bound within our space and time.

It is also pointless to think of endless years stretching on and on in which God was all by himself until *one day* he decided to make a world. There are no days or years except as God creates them. He stands outside the limits of time and space. Time stretches endlessly to the past, so far back at least, that we can never get to a beginning.

The important consideration, therefore, is not the insoluble riddle of time's beginning and time's end, but learning to be conscious of the kind of time in which we live. We are confined within the limits of the living present. Time comes to us out of the unknown future and recedes into the unalterable past. Here we stand and must make our decisions. We can never actually jump ahead into the future or somehow get back again into the past. We can only *think* ahead of the future and *think* back to and remember the past. But God stands above and beyond the whole course of history. He is in a position to see and know all things. (This is what is meant by his omniscience.)

THE DEPENDABILITY OF CREATION

God in his love has created a wonderful dependability in nature itself, so that we can depend upon the sun's regular rising and the steady course of the stars, and the regular and fruitful return of the seasons. This is symbolized by the rainbow in the sky (Genesis 9:12-17). Without the dependable order of nature active, purposeful living would be impossible. If we could not depend on the order of the world, if the world were just topsy-turvy, the plaything of all kinds of demons and spirits, we could plant no crops, build no bridges, play no games.

When we think about the many puzzling disorders in the world, such as storms and other natural catastrophes, we must be humble. In part it is only our ignorance that we can't see the dependable order in the disorder. Even the storm brings its benefits. In part there is an insoluble mystery of evil connected with the disorders of creation from which the creation itself groans to be freed (Romans 8:18-25). It is a mark of real trust in the love of the Creator God not to let such catastrophe cause us to forsake him. A person who really trusts another trusts him even when the going is rough and when evidence seems to go against him.

THE MASKS OF CREATION

The sun, the rain, and the good earth—all of nature in its beauty and endless fertility—are filled with God's presence (Acts 14; Psalms 19 and 104). They are the means God uses to provide us with light, warmth, and food. God never gives us anything directly, but always through a medium. In this medium, however, he is immediately present to us. Luther refers to the media God uses as the "masks of creation." The sun reflects God's selfless love, because it gets nothing for its shining but is burning itself out for man. The same is true of plants that yield their fruit and animals that yield patiently to the yoke and give their lives that men may live. All the riches of the earth—which not only sustain man's life but also make it possible to create beautiful things and to provide all kinds of enjoyable and delightful pleasures — all these are masks behind which and in which is found the God of love.

THE APPROPRIATENESS OF THE CREATED WORLD

Finally, we should note how wonderfully God has structured the world to make it a fit theater for the realization of his purpose, life-together-in-love. God made man male and female, giving them to each other to create the human family. This was a work of love which brings men together in love.

The fact that man is made in God's image means not only that man has mental powers superior to those of animals, but also that he is the kind of being who can love as God loves. This love finds its first and most intimate expression in the family. Here the differences between male and female make possible a life of mutual service where each serves the other with unique gifts. Though all men are equal in God's sight and all equally beloved of him, they are not alike. The differences between them are God-willed so that they can serve each other in love. They are thus brought together for a life of mutual love, not only in the family but also in the community of work where men serve each other with their gifts. All the rich variety of human living together is rooted here. What a drab world this would be if all men were the same, alike in looks, talents, and personalities! Thank God for the color, the diversity, the rich variety of men and women and races and people in the world, which makes possible our exciting life of work, play, song, arts, and worship.

Despite the evils in the world, the inexplicable tragedies, the awful consequences of willful sin, God's love should not be sold short when presenting the doctrine of creation. God made man for joy and for blessedness, and all man's life should be one great song of joy. Yet man should not lose his heart to the world. He is to love God supremely as the giver of every good and perfect gift, not the gift itself; just as the bride is to love the bridegroom and not the ring with which he adorns her finger. Without being sentimental, and fully aware of the evils in nature and the ambiguity of the witness, the possibilities that God provides in his love dare not be minimized. If the gifts are there as real gifts, the responsibility to use them rightly is increased. The great temptation is always to neglect personal gifts, to plunder and abuse the riches of creation, to allow time and talents to be wasted. Youth, therefore, should be challenged to its full potential. This is more urgent when the great, great needs of the world are realized. They are to share in God's great work in providing for these needs. Every child of God is also to be a mask of God in and through which he blesses men.

With this kind of emphasis on the loving God of creation, it will then not be difficult to lead the pupils to a sense of sin and the need of forgiveness and renewed strength in order to fulfill an obligation. In short, you will be building a solid foundation for the detailed study next year of the God of redemption.

Prayer and the Lord's Prayer

By Edgar M. Carlson

During this course you will be guiding your class in a study of prayer. If you succeed in helping each pupil to develop a deeper understanding of prayer and to cultivate a proper attitude toward prayer, you will have made a lasting contribution to his growth as a Christian. If you fail—well, you must not!

Surely the first step in such preparation is to pray. If you cannot, or do not pray, nothing that you say will be very convincing. So do not undertake to teach any lesson without having prepared yourself by careful study of the lesson materials, and by personal prayer. Your pupils are not only learners, but also persons whose individual needs and family situations you should know well. Pray for each one in terms of his own problems and needs. Make your lesson preparation an occasion for meditation on the Scripture passages involved, with prayer for insight and understanding. You are not only a teacher, but a Christian in the process of becoming a more effective witness.

WHAT IS PRAYER?

Let us try this as a definition: "Prayer is conversation with God." Children who are in the habit of "saying their prayers" will understand that definition. Young children feel quite free in their conversations with God. They tell him what they want, who is sick, and almost anything that comes to mind. They may think of the conversation more in terms of talking than of listening. So it is important to help your pupils to understand that prayer is listening, too. And they need to learn how and where to listen for God's answers.

If we are to think of prayer as "conversation," we must understand that we are addressing a person. If God is thought of as an impersonal force, prayer will lose its vitality and its urgency. We must understand, too, that this person is our friend. We may converse, when we have to, with the bill collector or the bully in the school yard, but prayer is not and should not be that kind of reluctant conversation. As you study the Lord's Prayer with your pupils you will be emphasizing how much the Father cares for them. We know that God is our friend because we know that he is "the Father of our Lord Jesus Christ."

Thinking of prayer as "conversation" also should make clear that it is not just asking for things. What kind of a relationship would there be between friends if they never spoke to each other except when they asked for favors? They share their joys as well as their worries. They express their gratitude; they commend and compliment one another. Of course, one must remember that prayer is not a conversation between equals. God is not a "buddy" or a "chum"; he is "Lord of lords and King of kings." We must have respect for him, and our conversation should be earnest and sincere.

Let us try another definition: "Prayer is what you want most out of life." Sometimes this is referred to as the "master motive." In this sense everyone prays. If one's top ambition in life is to become rich, or to become famous, or to be popular, or to serve his fellow men, then this is his real prayer. It is important that your pupils begin to understand this. They should not be talking to God only about the little things, but also about the big things. Regardless of what it is they want out of life, they should begin praying about it. If it isn't good enough or big enough to talk over with God, it isn't good enough or big enough to be their life's ambition.

Maybe this isn't a definition, but it needs to be said: "Prayer should be the first step, instead of the last stand." Most everyone prays when things get bad enough. When the outlook is dark, when a loved one is seriously ill, when the situation gets desperate—people pray. When there doesn't seem to be any other place to go than to our knees, we are willing to try prayer. God does not forsake us in these extremities and we ought to call upon him. But prayer should come at the beginning of the enterprise instead of at the end. At the beginning of a job, the opening of a day, the start of a project—this is the time to come to God in prayer. It will purify our motives, clarify our values, and even make us more efficient and effective in our work.

WHAT IS THE USE OF PRAYING?

That is putting it rather crassly. It would be more proper to speak of "the values of prayer." But the question is phrased this way on purpose to raise some doubt as to whether prayer should ever be evaluated in terms of what we get out of it. As persons it is our nature to communicate with other persons. This communication makes life rich and full; we would be greatly impoverished if we could not participate in the lives of others in this way. Yet we do not require this kind of conversation to justify itself in terms of what we get out of it.

We should pray because God is God and we are his creatures; he is our Father and we are his children. We want to communicate with him. And so our lives are greatly enriched by prayer, especially when we do not use it as a means to enrich ourselves.

What are some of the ways in which our lives are enriched? For one thing, prayer puts us in a receptive mood so that God's blessing can come to us. We stop the wheels of our minds and focus attention upon God. We become aware of him and of his will. Our minds can be wholly absorbed with worldly things so that God doesn't have a chance to command our attention. What chance would any friendship have if we never gave a thought to the friend or loved one? God's blessing may come to us in many ways through those moments of contact that we have with him in prayer. Perhaps we are made sensitive to some wrong in our lives, our consciences may be pricked, we may gain some fresh assurance of the goodness of God, a deeper recognition of how dependent we are on him. Or we may escape from that selfishness which threatens our intimate relationship with him.

Also, our motives and wants are held up to the light of God's will. That is why it is so important that we should pray for the things we want most, regardless of what they may be. You can't hold up an unholy, self-centered ambition to God day after day in prayer without its changing into something for which you can honestly and respectably seek his endorsement and support. Sometimes just putting our wants and desires into words helps us to see how unworthy they are. This is especially true if we put them into words which we intend to present before God.

There can be no doubt that prayer does things *to* us and to our relationships with others. For instance, if there is someone that you do not like, or perhaps even hate, start praying regularly for him. You will find that it isn't possible to keep on hating someone that you are praying for. You won't be able even to snub him, or to say nasty things about him. Prayer can help break down seemingly impenetrable barriers between you and others. On the other hand, if there is someone that you really care for and want to help, try praying for him. See how your mutual understanding will grow and your imagination quicken as you become alert to opportunities to prove yourself his friend.

DOES PRAYER "CHANGE THINGS"?

Can we really believe that prayer will accomplish things *for* us? Does prayer really "change things"? The answer is surely "Yes." The real basis for believing it is the promise of Jesus. Prayer is something that we believe in, not something that we prove. All kinds of testimonies have been given by earnest Christians concerning the power of prayer, but these may not convince the unbeliever.

Usually it is possible to give some other interpretation to the events that seem to a Christian to be a result of prayer. Perhaps the doctor's diagnosis was wrong, and the patient suffering from what was considered to be a fatal illness recovered. Perhaps it was just a coincidence that the rains came when the drought was on the verge of ruining the crops. God does not force people to believe in the power of prayer by bludgeoning their minds with "proofs."

We can understand a little about how prayer brings power into our own lives. When we make our prayers and our ambitions coincide, then we harness all of our own resources behind our prayers; we accomplish more than we can when our interests are moving in all directions. But we also put ourselves at the disposal of God so that the power of his Spirit can multiply our own efforts in his cause. When we work at the things which God wants done in the world, we can be sure that we are working with him, and he with us.

One of the big questions concerning prayer is whether God can intervene in our world in ways that we do not understand to accomplish his purposes. The Christian believes in the possibility of such intervention. He knows that God works through others—doctors, parents, persons in every calling—to bless men. But we do not believe that the God who raised Christ from the dead and who will raise us from death to eternal life with him is limited by what human help he can command for making this a better world. His resources are greater than all of our resources combined. In this confidence, we pray for the unlikely and the impossible, knowing that "all things are possible with God."

But there is a problem that rises in connection with our understanding of the world as governed by natural laws. The various sciences that have catalogued these laws seem to say that everything that takes place in the natural world can be accounted for by these "laws of nature." Doesn't this limit what God can do? What is the use of praying if things happen because of a built-in necessity? Of course, the Christian accepts the validity of all the facts that science has discovered. He sees in these laws of nature a description of God's characteristic way of acting. Our God is not a capricious God who puts the sun in orbit only when he feels like it. The regularity and orderliness of the natural universe is an evidence of God's reliability. He works through his natural laws.

Many dedicated scientists agree that there is more about the world that they do not know and understand than there is that they do know and understand. Some things about it cannot be classified and catalogued and explained by known laws. And the Christian will be very skeptical of any attempt to imprison God in his universe. Even if the whole of creation and all creatures should be strictly limited by the laws of nature, the Creator is above his creation. We cannot limit him by telling him what he can and cannot do.

Another problem of prayer concerns the vastness of the universe and the number of people in it. How can God be concerned about my personal needs and problems? This is as though the mother of one child should wonder how the mother of seven could love them all as much as she loves her only child. Where love is involved, numbers do not seem to matter. Jesus said that no sparrow falls to the ground without the Father's knowledge; the hairs of our heads are all numbered by him. We need have no fear that the God of infinite wisdom and boundless love will overlook our most personal needs.

33

But where shall we look for the answer to our prayers? Often, if we pray as Jesus taught us, God will help us to find the answer in ourselves. It may be a strengthened resolution to do the right, a greater capacity for getting along with people, an inner peace and calm. Sometimes his answer will come through others, perhaps our parents or friends. More often we should expect to find the answer in the Bible. Here God speaks. If we want to know his will, we should listen to what he has to say. And sometimes we must expect the answer to be "No." God cares for us too much to give us everything that we ask for.

WHAT IS CHRISTIAN ABOUT PRAYER?

Obviously, Christians are not the only ones who pray. All religious people pray, whether they are Buddhists, Moslems, ancestor worshipers, primitive animists, or Christians. Even irreligious people are likely to pray in times of real distress. All humans are limited and dependent. When the disciples asked Jesus to teach them to pray (Luke 11:1), it was not because they had never learned to pray. It was because they wanted to be able to pray as Jesus did, with the same sense of the Father's presence and with the same conviction that their petitions were heard by him. There should be as much difference between the prayers of Christians and non-Christians as there is between their lives. If there isn't much difference in their prayers, there is probably little difference in their lives.

The most general and inclusive counsel Jesus gave with regard to a Christian's praying is that it should be "in my name" (read John 14:13, 14). This means that we should pray for those things which we believe Jesus would want us to have, the petitions to which he would sign his name. We should pray in the same spirit of submission that Jesus had to the Father's will. "Not my will, but thine, be done," he prayed in the Garden of Gethsemane. We should pray with the same confidence in God's power and goodness which Jesus had and which is guaranteed for us by his own death and resurrection.

The most complete and detailed instruction which Jesus gave concerning prayer was the prayer which he taught his disciples—the "Lord's Prayer." The prayer did not get its name because it was a prayer which Jesus prayed. He would not have needed to pray for forgiveness of his trespasses. There is no indication anywhere in the Gospels that Jesus had any sense of guilt. On the contrary, he said, "Which of you convicts me of sin?" (John 8:46). It is the "Lord's Prayer" because it is the prayer he taught and the pattern of praying he suggested we use.

THE LORD'S PRAYER

The Bible contains two versions of the Lord's Prayer. Matthew's version is the most complete; it is the source of the form which we use

(Matthew 6:9–13). The only difference is that Matthew uses the word "debts" instead of "trespasses." The word "trespasses" may have been drawn from the verses which follow (6:14–15). In this same part of the prayer, Luke uses the word "sins" (Luke 11:1–4). You may wish to call attention to the New English Bible, which translates Matthew's word as "wrongs." There need not be any difference in meaning between "debts" (considered to be moral debts) and "trespasses" or "sins," but it may properly be asked why different words should be used since the prayer appears to have been memorized and repeated regularly. The answer probably lies in the fact that Jesus spoke in Aramaic, the common language of his time and place, and the Gospels were written in Greek. Matthew and Luke, or the sources from which they drew, used different Greek words to translate Jesus' original Aramaic word.

The Doxology, "for Thine is the kingdom, and the power, and the glory, forever and ever," was probably not a part of the prayer as Jesus taught it. It may have been a response spoken or sung by the worshipers when the prayer was used. There are close parallels to this kind of prayer ending in Jewish worship; it would have been very natural for Jewish Christians to respond in this way to the prayer of our Lord. The Doxology may be thought of as a contribution which the church has made to the Lord's Prayer and which sums up the faith in which the church has prayed throughout the centuries. The Doxology appears as a part of the prayer very early in the history of the church in the so-called Teaching of the Twelve Apostles from around the year A.D. 100.

There are substantial differences between Matthew's version of the prayer and Luke's. The setting is different. In Matthew it is included as a part of the Sermon on the Mount; in Luke it is an answer to a specific request from one of the disciples: "Lord, teach us to pray, as John taught his disciples." The occasion for the question was that Jesus had been praying "in a certain place," and his disciples had been impressed by the way he prayed. The differences are clearly seen when the two versions are placed side by side.

MATTHEW

Our Father who art in heaven,
Hallowed be thy name.
Thy kingdom come,
Thy will be done,
 On earth as it is in heaven.
Give us this day our daily bread;
And forgive us our debts,
 As we also have forgiven our
  debtors;
And lead us not into temptation,
 But deliver us from evil.

LUKE

Father,
hallowed be thy name.
Thy kingdom come.

Give us each day our daily bread; and forgive us our sins, for we ourselves forgive everyone who is indebted to us; and lead us not into temptation.

How shall we account for these differences and what shall we say about them? Would we not expect the Bible to quote Jesus accurately and would not the Gospel accounts then agree as to exactly what he said? This might give a good occasion to help your students understand how the New Testament was formed. (Especially if they raise questions about it.) The books of the New Testament were written quite a few years after Jesus' death. There were some letters to young congregations written by Paul and other leaders of the early church. There seem to have been some early records of the life and teachings of Christ, but these were not stenographic accounts of what Jesus said and did. Possibly, there were also collections of his sayings that were circulated among the churches. Generally, people remembered and repeated what he said. They preached about him and his message. Some of these sermons are preserved in the Book of Acts. When the Gospels were written, they were not intended primarily as biographies of Jesus or historical records. They were preaching documents, designed to persuade readers that Jesus was indeed the Christ. (The word "gospel" itself means "good news.") The writer of John's Gospel makes it very explicit: "Now Jesus did many other signs in the presence of the disciples, which are not written in this book; but these are written that you may believe that Jesus is the Christ, the Son of God, and that believing you may have life in his name" (John 20:30, 31).

Therefore, the writers collected material in the manner which best served their purpose, somewhat as a preacher does in preparing a sermon. Some scholars think the Sermon on the Mount, in which Matthew includes the Lord's Prayer, was originally a collection of sayings. It is, of course, also possible that Jesus repeated his teachings. A good teacher will often say the same thing in different words on separate occasions. It is also possible that the "oral tradition" did not always retain everything just as Jesus had said it. Thus, the phrase "thy will be done on earth as it is in heaven" may have dropped out of Luke's source as being merely a repetition of "thy kingdom come"; the same could be said of the omission of "but deliver us from the evil one." (In part, it repeats the petition which precedes it, "Lead us not into temptation.") At any rate, we need not be disturbed about variations in the biblical accounts. For some reason, Luke did not include the whole prayer. We can be glad that Matthew gave it in full.

Now let us look more carefully at the Lord's Prayer. You will note that there is a certain parallelism between the structure of the Commandments and the structure of the Lord's Prayer. Just as the first three commandments deal with our relation to God in terms of obligation, so the first three petitions deal with our relation to God in terms of our earnest hope and desire. What we are there commanded to do, we here pray that we might do. Both have as their objective the proper relationship between man and God. The remaining petitions of the Lord's Prayer deal with our life in this world, just as the remaining commandments deal with our relations to others in this world. (Note the change in the pronouns from "thy" to "us": "thy name"—"thy kingdom"—"thy will"; "give us"—"forgive us"—"lead us"—"deliver us.") One should not try to relate the petitions individually to the commandments—although there is a direct parallel between "Thou shalt not take the name of the Lord thy God in vain" and "Hallowed be thy name." The person who earnestly prays these petitions will be a person who obeys the Ten Commandments.

It is important to keep clearly in mind to whom we are addressing this prayer. You should be helping your pupils to a larger and deeper understanding of God through this course. A small, indifferent God can only lead to small, indifferent prayers. We have a great God and should have great expectations, leading us to great prayers. "Our Father, who art in heaven." Every word there is important.

The God to whom we pray is not a private God; he is the God and Father of all men. He is the only God. We must not think of him as a personal bank account on which we can draw for the realization of our personal ambitions and selfish desires. He is not obligated to us; we are obligated to him. He is not dependent on us; we are dependent on him. He is "the Father Almighty, Maker of heaven and earth," as we confess in the First Article of the Creed. Listen to some of the doxologies from the New Testament: ". . . the blessed and only Sovereign, the King of kings and Lord of lords, who alone has immortality and dwells in unapproachable light, whom no man has seen or can see" (1 Timothy 6:15, 16); "Great and wonderful are thy deeds, O Lord God the Almighty! Just and true are thy ways, O King of the ages! Who shall not fear and glorify thy name, O Lord?" (Revelation 15:3, 4). It is to him that we pray. We are entering into the presence of "the Majesty on high." Indeed, "Hallowed [holy] be thy name"!

The reason we dare to enter the presence of God is that we know that he is the "Father of our Lord Jesus Christ" and, therefore, also our Father. We know the love which Jesus had for us is indeed the love of God. We have seen "the light of the knowledge of the glory of God in the face of Jesus Christ" (2 Corinthians 4:6). It is Jesus who has shown us "the Father." "He that has seen me has seen the Father" (John 14:9). We should, therefore, come to God in the same spirit and with the same boldness with which we would come to Jesus.

Another major idea with which the teacher should be familiar is the "kingdom of God." This concept runs all the way through the Bible. It is a basic idea in Jesus' teaching and in his understanding of his mission. In this respect Jesus was clearly building on the Old Testament.

Briefly, the basic element in the concept of the "kingdom of God" is "the rule of God" or "the realm of God." God should rule in his world. To belong to the rule or realm of God is to be obedient to his will. The kingdom is a relationship more than a place. The idea that God was the rightful ruler over the people is often asserted in the Old Testament.

When Moses led the slaves out of Egypt he welded them into a "covenant people." Jehovah would be their God and they would be his people. This sounded fine, but through the years of being ruled by judges and kings (many of them imperfect and even hostile to the will of God) the Israelites became a wayward people. The people believed that David was a great king because he brought honor and glory to their nation. So it is no wonder that they looked back upon the rule of David as the good old days. Sometimes they hoped for another ruler, a "son of David," who should measure up to their great hero-king. Then all the problems would vanish and a new spiritual vigor and unity would come to the land. The prophets doubted that the whole nation could be in fact "a people of God." They put their faith in a faithful remnant. Even this seemed futile and their hope came to center more and more on a great messianic leader who would come to deliver the people and establish a kingdom of righteousness.

When John the Baptist began his preaching by the River Jordan, he told the people that the kingdom of God was at hand. When Jesus began his ministry, Matthew says, "he went about all Galilee, teaching in their synagogues and preaching the gospel of the kingdom" (Matthew 4:23). Jesus spoke of his kingdom as something that had come with him. It was now here (Luke 11:20). People entered this kingdom by their childlike faith in him rather than by their nationality (Mark 10:14). Jesus often spoke of the kingdom as a precious possession, like a pearl, or a treasure hidden in a field (Matthew 13:44-46).

In one sense, Jesus brought the kingdom with him because in him God ruled completely. He was wholly subject to the Father's will. "I seek not my own will but the will of him who sent me" (John 5:30). He is the only complete instance of "the rule of God" which history offers. But he is not only a man who is ruled by God; he is also the God who rules. Jesus is the incarnate Son of God. When men believe in Christ and follow him they are in the right relationship to God. To pray "Thy will be done" is to pray that we may be in that kind of relationship.

So one may think of Jesus and those who gather about him to listen, believe, and obey as being the "kingdom of God." They have the kingdom in their hearts. If the kingdom was present in the world it was because Jesus, the Son of God, was present. Don't miss the fact that the New Testament stresses the kingdom as a growing community of faith and obedience. To pray "Thy kingdom come" is to ask that this growth continue, that it include us and all mankind. Many of Jesus' parables of the kingdom emphasize this growth from small beginnings— a grain of mustard seed that grows into a tree, a piece of leaven that leavens the whole lump of dough.

Although the kingdom included both Jesus and his disciples, there was a difference between them. In Jesus the rule of God was firm and sure; in the disciples it was a frail, flickering thing. They hardly knew whether they dared to believe in him. When he was arrested and imprisoned, their fears got the best of them. When he died it seemed as though it was all over. But with the resurrection their faith revived and they gradually came to understand how he had triumphed over death and every enemy of man. His love had triumphed over the evil in men's hearts and he had borne "our sins in his body on the tree." Now nothing could separate them from this love of God in Christ. The kingdom had indeed been established in the world. It was "the kingdom of his beloved Son, in whom we have redemption, the forgiveness of sins" (Colossians 1:13, 14).

But the disciples also understood that this kingdom, this rule of God, was not yet fully realized in this world. Christ had overcome his enemies and all the enemies of God, but they were still at large in the world. Sin and death were still here. Yet the kingdom was still coming in its fullness. And Jesus would come again. He had won the decisive battle and he would win the war. There is no longer a question about the outcome of this conflict. God will triumph. Those who are members of his kingdom will triumph, too, even though like him they must die and be raised again.

When we pray that God's kingdom may come, we pray that God may have his way with us, that we may respond to his gospel in faith and obedience, that we may have fellowship with God through Jesus Christ here and now, that we may have a sure hope of an eternal life beyond all our tomorrows.

In describing the biblical idea of the "kingdom of God" we introduced another note which deserves further comment. The "kingdom of God" is set over against another kingdom, the kingdom of the world. God's kingdom is established not in neutral territory, but in enemy country. The world that God created has been taken over by the Evil One. The conflict between Jesus and the powers of this world led to his death. He saw it not only as a conflict with individuals who disagreed with him or were hostile to him; he said "now shall the ruler of this world be cast out" (John 12:31). The devil was very real to Jesus, as he was to the early Christians. Paul said, ". . . we are not contending against flesh and blood, but against the principalities, against the powers, against the world rulers of this present darkness, against the spiritual hosts of wickedness in the heavenly places" (Ephesians 6:12). The Lord's Prayer is intended for soldiers engaged in a battle against evil—indeed, against the Evil One. We must guard against temptations and snares set by the enemy. We must pray for deliverance, for the enemy is stronger than we are—but not stronger than our Lord. We must not think of evil simply as sickness or poverty or other misfortune.

In teaching this course there will be fine opportunity to make clear the place that forgiveness has in our Christian experience. The pupils need to learn that they must not allow anything to come between them and God. When we are selfish, mean, unkind, and inconsiderate we set up a barrier between ourselves and God. We try to hide our true selves from him. But we are invited to pray for forgiveness, and forgiveness wipes out the barrier. Even when we do our best to let God have his way with us, we do not fully succeed. This will always be true; we will always have to live by forgiveness. We must do our best to be obedient, but our assurance of membership in the kingdom must always rest on the grace of "forgiveness" of God. And to live by forgiveness means that we must be forgiving people. Else we are not sincere.

Just one final thought—think about the pronouns in the Lord's Prayer again. Notice how many of them are plural. Although prayer is a very personal thing, and we should not hesitate to ask for the most personal and specific needs, including daily bread and all the things necessary for our physical existence and well-being, we must remember not to approach God for ourselves alone. We must think about all who need daily bread, if our prayer for daily bread is to follow the pattern which Jesus gave us. So, too, we must be concerned about the trespasses of others, and the temptations and dangers which others face. We pray as members of a Christian community when we pray the Lord's Prayer.

SECTION 3

SECTION THREE

Teaching Plans for Term One

UNIT A:
introduction to confirmation

UNIT OBJECTIVES

1. To help the pupil feel the importance of confirmation.

2. To help him feel more at home in the worship and life of the congregation.

3. To deepen his understanding of his church in its missionary, educational and worship activities.

SCOPE OF UNIT

This unit introduces the three-year course that lies ahead. It might therefore be approached by a "So you're going to be confirmed" motif. What's involved in such a step? What's expected of a confirmand?

In rather broad strokes you will cover such areas as: what it means to be a Christian; the life, history, and work of the congregation; dominant features of the Lutheran church; and the worship of the Lutheran church.

Some of these areas, such as the church and worship, will be studied in greater depth later. Therefore your scope will be limited to studies that will make the pupil feel more at home and encourage him to take a more active role in the congregation.

The local congregation is the starting point, since the pupil will view the church in terms of his own congregation—its building and personnel and program and worship and structure. Even the wider work of the church is seen against the backdrop of the congregation's involvement in this wider church.

STRUCTURE OF THE UNIT

Four sessions are planned for this unit (five if your year runs beyond the thirty-session span). No rigid limits are placed on the sessions themselves. If suggestions for a session prove to be too full or interesting to compress within the allotted time, continue them into the next session. If suggestions seem too sparse, don't hesitate to launch into material suggested for the following session. A wide latitude is allowed, so long as the unit itself does not reach beyond the four- or five-session limit.

Suggestions for each session include such activities as research projects, Bible study, pupil reports and discussion, use of chapters in the pupil's book.

Certain things may be expected of pupils beyond the class sessions. This should be made clear at the outset of the unit. Requirements may include regular attendance at public worship (report on the sermon, if this is a congregation's practice), daily Bible reading, reading of the pupil's book, or participation in research projects. The full value of this course hinges on pupil activity between sessions.

MATERIALS NEEDED

A considerable variety of materials will be needed for this unit. Time will be needed to assemble them, but it will be time well spent. As a check list, the following are suggested:

Bibles (preferably the Revised Standard Version) for all sessions.

Service Book and Hymnal *for most sessions (one per pupil).*

Constitution and Parish Register of your congregation.

Brochures on the history of your congregation and on its personnel, organizations, activities, and finances.

Brochures and leaflets describing the wider work of the church, especially foreign and home missions, inner-mission agencies and institutions, and colleges and seminaries.

Since many of these materials will be used for research projects they should be available at the first session and, if possible, arranged on a display table for pupils to borrow. Usually the pastor will have many of these materials on hand.

RESEARCH PROJECTS

Motivation is important in launching and continuing research projects. While most of the research projects suggested have a built-in appeal, some are better suited to special aptitudes and interests of individual students.

The research projects suggested can be handled in a number of ways. The whole class may work on them either before or during the session; individual pupils may present a written report on their projects by the end of the unit; or, if your year runs beyond the thirty-session span, an entire session may be devoted to them. However, they are most effective when worked into the sessions themselves. Use the method best suited to the time available and progress of your own class.

Materials for the projects should be readily available to pupils. If the pastor conducts this opening unit, the lay teacher may conduct the "project area," guiding pupils in their research and providing materials for their use. The pastor's file is a handy source of needed materials.

Manual or Newspaper

Pupils may be asked to assemble their findings from session projects (see below) for the preparation of a manual or newspaper about their church. If multiple copies are projected, arrangements should be made for duplicating. If the findings prove of value for a wider audience, arrangements can be made for making a manual or newspaper available to the whole congregation.

In this project the four categories suggested for session research could provide general areas for the manual. A group of pupils could serve as an editorial committee to determine how much information to include. Artistic-minded pupils could provide sketches of the church building and its significant elements.

Pupils themselves should determine the form and motif of their research projects. A "did you know" type of treatment could be suggested, such as:

Did you know that all Lutherans in America lined up side by side would stretch more than 2000 miles? That one out of every . . . persons you pass on the street is a Lutheran? That there are . . . churches within one mile of our church? That . . . per cent of our members are in positions of leadership in our church?

Roving Reporter

Private research projects may be undertaken by "roving reporters." Their task will be to ferret out information through interviews with members of the church. Some guidance may be given them on phrasing questions, whom to interview, and how to get information. In some cases they can conduct a public opinion poll within the congregation; in other cases, they can interview young people of other churches; in still other cases, they will get information from more seasoned leaders of the church. *Their work should be supplementary to the group project.*

In assembling data on local history, the roving reporter can determine what facts and events the members of the congregation regard as most important. He can do the same for other areas, discovering what the members do not know about church finances, the wider work of the church, and the work of the local congregation.

As many as ten or twelve pupils could serve in this capacity, working in pairs or singly. Their fields of investigation should be limited so that their work can be completed within your four or five sessions.

Special Projects for Individual Sessions

The session plans will spell out other project possibilities at the point of assignment and use in class. The topics considered in these projects are:

Sessions 1 and 2: Administration and records.
Session 2: History of the congregation.
Session 3: Personnel and organizations.
Session 4: Worship, finances, and the church at large.

---

session 1
SCOPE OF SESSION

Much of this session will be devoted to achieving a deeper understanding of the meaning of confirmation and to motivate pupils toward
confirmation. It will be a "get acquainted" session which provides a
preview of the three-year study ahead.

MATERIALS NEEDED

Pupil's book. Bibles. Pencils and paper. The Order for Confirmation
in the *Service Book and Hymnal*. Research materials. The congregation's
constitution. A variety of brochures for future research projects.

AN OVERVIEW OF THE SESSION

1. Get personal data from pupils.
*2. Distribute the pupil's books. Using the pupil's book as a guide,
outline the scope and design of the course.*
*3. Explain any specific requirements or expectations (such as
attendance at public worship, daily Bible reading, or study of the
pupil's book).*
*4. Discuss the significance of confirmation, centering on why
pupils want to be confirmed and what confirmation means to them.*
*5. Explore Bible passages dealing with the sterner demands of
discipleship.*
*6. Outline research projects for coming sessions; ask for volunteers
as "roving reporters."*
7. Make assignments for the next session.

SESSION PLAN IN GREATER DETAIL

1. Get information.

Presumably you are already acquainted with pupils in your class.
If you wish some vital statistics for records, gather information quickly
on slips of paper. Information usually requested includes full name,
address, birth date, parents' names and church affiliation, school and
grade, phone, date and place of baptism (if known). You may also
want to know:

How long has pupil lived in the neighborhood?

Attendance patterns in the Sunday church school? At services? In other schools of the church?

Brothers and sisters? Where does the pupil stand in his family?

Range of interests: sports, music, reading, hobbies?

Their present link with the church is focal here. Later patterns of church loyalty are often related to present family patterns or to patterns set by other young people. Make sure that you get to know each pupil personally. As a teacher you are helping him grow and develop as a Christian according to his own capabilities.

2. Distribute the pupil's books and introduce the course.

Material in Section One to this teacher's guide will be of help as you introduce the course. Help the pupils see that the pattern for the three years is a balance between "I Believe" and "I Respond." Opening terms of each year sound the former theme, second terms the latter.

To outline this pattern in greater detail, have pupils turn to the *Small Catechism* in the back of their books. Articles of the Creed are first-term concerns of all three years, with other parts of the Catechism providing the "I Respond" concerns. Thus, the first year examines faith in God and the First Article, balanced in the second term by the response of prayer, with emphasis on the Lord's Prayer and worship. The second year considers belief in Christ and the Second Article, with the response emphasizing the Ten Commandments as guideposts for Christian living. The third year studies the role of the Holy Spirit and the Third Article, the sacraments of Baptism and the Lord's Supper, with a full review of what it means to live as a confirmed member of the church in the concluding term.

3. Explain specific requirements.

Some idea of week-to-week expectations could be given here. Don't make requirements too overpowering, but be sure pupils understand them. They may include: regular attendance at Sunday church school and worship; daily Bible reading, using passages appointed in the pupil's book; regular reading of chapters in the pupil's book prior to class sessions. Appeal also to pupils to assume responsibility for research projects. If they feel that their reports are vital to the success of the sessions, they will probably respond more earnestly.

4. Discuss the significance of confirmation.

You may ask pupils to write down what confirmation means to them (perhaps while they are filling out their personal information sheets). Ask them to write what they think, not what they think you'd like to read. Why do they want to be confirmed?

Use the chalkboard to put their reasons before them. You may get such answers as: "Because my parents want me to be confirmed"; "Because kids my age are being confirmed"; "Because it's the thing to do"; "Because I want to commune"; "Because I'd like to be a full part of the church." Reasons may not go deep or may reflect a choice not their own; but you'll know where each pupil stands and how much attention each must be given to raise his motivation. Help the group evaluate the list of reasons and sort out the most important.

The term "confirmation" deserves some treatment. What do pupils associate with it? Apart from its church use, what does "to confirm" mean? What is being assured, sealed?

Why do we speak of *being* confirmed? Who does the confirming? You may indicate how in some churches confirmation is reserved for the bishop in his annual visit, and how in our church the act is performed by the pastor. In such instances, the church as an agent of God confirms the baptism of the individual into the church of God. Underscore God's role in the whole process—how he adopted the child into his holy family at baptism—how he has brought the youth to this point by constant, careful nurture. God uses parents and sponsors and teachers and worship —all as tools for nurture. Thus, confirmation is not so much the pupil's choice, as God's continual call.

In this connection read over the Order for Confirmation. Ask pupils to give careful attention to:

a) *The linking of confirmation with baptism as though one were the extension of the other. Make sure that the pastor knows the pupils who are not baptized so that arrangements for the sacrament can be made.*

b) *The use of the Apostles' Creed as a means by which faith is professed.*

c) *Promises of faithfulness to the Christian faith, to the church, to the Means of Grace.*

d) *The prayer for the gift of the Holy Spirit.*

e) *The blessing, with its emphasis on the Spirit's work within.*

f) *A reception into full active membership in the family of believers.*

Chapter 1 of the pupil's book raises questions about the pupil's impression of a confirmation service. (In this session time may be provided for a silent reading of Chapter 1.) Ask pupils to describe their impressions, if they have attended such a service. Do these impressions tie in with those of Chapter 1?

Further discussion can proceed on the description in the pupil's book of what a Christian really is, and of what is involved in a profession of faith. Ask pupils how they would define a Christian. Is there anything that sets him apart from others? Any outward marks? Could their definition apply equally to a Buddhist? Is there such a thing as "the Christian thing to do"? Or does the term "Christian" apply only to a person, never to a thing?

Guide the pupils into sharpening their definition, lest the term be used loosely. People sometimes identify it with a social grace or an attitude—like honesty or courtesy. A merchant will be courteous; it's good business. But courtesy itself does not imply that he is a Christian. Thus, Christians will be honest and courteous; but not all who are courteous and honest are necessarily Christian.

The note of personal commitment looms large here. No one can be confirmed for another. The faith each professes, even though voiced in the ancient form of the Creed, must still be personal. Underscore this as the one human qualification for confirmation.

5. Explore Bible passages.

If there is time, guide the pupils in exploring certain Bible passages which have a common theme of the sternness of Jesus' qualifications for discipleship. You could use passages such as:

Matthew 10:32–39 (What it means to accept Christ.)
Matthew 16:24–28 (The cost of discipleship.)
Luke 14:25–33 (Conditions of discipleship.)

Have the pupils read from their Bibles and note what Jesus required of his followers. After the passages have been read, ask the pupils for their reactions to the following statements:

Jesus isn't interested in having every Tom, Dick, and Harry as a follower.
Being a Christian isn't supposed to pay off.
Jesus might disrupt family relationships, rather than cement them.
Being a Christian means being a crepehanger, a killjoy.
Christianity ought to be more exclusive and snobbish, keeping people out who don't toe the line.
You can never really satisfy Jesus' requirements. Even your best isn't good enough.
Jesus is more interested in quality than quantity. He doesn't care how big the church is, so long as members are one hundred per cent committed.

6. Outline research projects for coming sessions.

You can let the pupils examine documents such as the congregation's constitution and the Parish Register to get a feeling of what makes their congregation what it is—a fellowship of people who believe in God through Christ. Let them look over the constitution of the congregation, noting what is included in the various articles such as: a doctrinal statement; membership in the larger body of Lutherans; kinds of members; requirements and duties of the pastor; duties of church councilmen; committees provided for; annual meeting. (You might provide mimeographed copies of the constitution for pupils to put in their notebooks.)

Let the pupils examine the Parish Register of the congregation to see the kinds of records kept for baptisms, weddings, funerals, and membership.

As an optional learning experience, if time permits, you could have the pupils prepare a list of service opportunities within their congregation, primarily for pupils their own age. Such a list may include helping in a nursery, preparing to teach a class, serving as an acolyte, taking the offering, serving as an officer of an organization, singing in choir, assisting in informal worship, caring for a church building, assisting in office work, or distributing literature or gifts to shut-ins. When such a list has been compiled, ask pupils to indicate their three special preferences.

Be sure to discuss procedures and personnel for research projects at the close of the session. You can bring to class materials related to the projects—brochures and pamphlets about the local church missionary work and the wider concerns of the church. Encourage the pupils to take materials home and bring in reports, written or verbal on dates which you set for reports.

7. Make assignments.

Assign the reading of Chapter 2 in the pupil's book (Chapter 1, too, if this has not been done in class). Ask the pupils to read the suggested Bible passages given in Chapter 2 at home on a daily schedule. Bible passages listed with the various chapters in the pupil's book are meant to be read prior to sessions in which the chapters are considered. Some attention may be given at this point to motivating this reading—locating passages in the pupil's book and raising a few questions about passages for Session 2. Such questions may be raised as: "Is the church really as important as some people think?" "What place does the church have in today's world?"

You can ask for volunteers, assign certain pupils or ask all pupils to delve into the history of your congregation. If an anniversary brochure has been prepared recently, this will provide each pupil with adequate material. Questions (you will need to tell them where they can find the answers) can be asked to sharpen their research. For example:

To what synod does the congregation belong?

Who have been pastors? Where did they come from? How long were they here? What terminated their pastorates?

What is the organization date? Where and under what circumstances did the congregation begin? Who were charter members?

When was the first building erected? Any other building programs since then?

What are the key events in the congregation's history?

What lay leaders should be remembered for significant service?

---

session 2
SCOPE OF SESSION

Session 2 focuses on the fellowship aspects of the church. It rests on the premise that confirmation brings a person into full communicant membership in the body of believers. The pupil should be guided to see the church as the body of Christ, a redeemed fellowship, instituted by God and empowered by His Holy Spirit.

MATERIALS NEEDED

Pupil's book. Bibles. The constitution of the congregation, the Parish Register. Materials needed for the research project.

AN OVERVIEW OF THE SESSION

1. Use the constitution of the congregation and the Parish Register to explore the procedures and requirements for persons to be received into the church.

2. Discuss the various meanings of "church," using Chapter 2 of the pupil's book as a resource for discussion.

3. Ask the pupils for their reaction to the idea that a Christian will want to align himself with the community of believers. What does the individual do for the church, and what does the church do for him?

4. Explore Bible passages in the pupil's book to determine the mission of the church and the character of the early church.

5. Turn to the research project, reporting on local history and discussing findings.

6. Make assignments for the next session.

SESSION PLAN IN GREATER DETAIL

1. How persons are received into church membership.

Let the pupils again examine the constitution of the congregation and the Parish Register to indicate ways by which persons affiliate with the church. These modes make it appear that membership is of one's free choice, like applying for club membership. Such a procedure is necessary. But much is at stake, for by this act God calls us into his church. Each person is a member at God's invitation.

Ask if this alters the pupil's ideas of church membership. Do we have a right to decide who is to belong and who isn't? Is the true basis for deciding whether *God* wants a person to belong? Do we really regard the church building as *God's* house, or the congregation as *God's* people?

If copies of synod minutes for a five- or ten-year period are available, ask some pupils to chart the comparisons of membership and financial statistics year by year, reported by their congregation. They will need some guidance both in locating the desired information and in understanding various categories (such as types of members or classifications of offerings).

2. Discuss the meanings of "church."

Reactions to the various roles and definitions in the pupil's book may launch this discussion. How does the pupil personally think of the church—as a four-walled building? As a group of somewhat like-minded people? Jot down on a chalkboard the pupils' ideas of what the word "church" means. You may get suggestions like these: a place of worship; a congregation; a building; a denomination; an institution of society; the "communion of saints" of the Apostles' Creed. Help the pupils to select the best ideas and form a working definition of the church. Do not tell them the answers you want. Lead them to develop their own understandings.

The two meanings of "church" that should stand out here are (*a*) the body of Christ and (*b*) the fellowship of believers. Other meanings are quite proper for certain purposes (like a building for worship, or an institution of society as are home and school). But these two meanings grow out of that basic relationship of people with Christ, and of people with other people through Christ. Because of this basic relationship congregations are formed, buildings erected, and worship conducted.

In most instances pupils wil regard themselves as "born" into the church. They feel no special call because they can't remember the day when they were outside the church. Should such a feeling lessen their appreciation? How do they regard their home—as something over which they exercised no choice? Or as a heritage they prize?

Discuss the various roles of the church, asking pupils to indicate which they consider central and which marginal. They may want to list various activities of the church, such as worship, teaching, fellowship, merciful service, singing, or crusades. Let them indicate what order of priority each activity would have.

3. A Christian and his church.

Ask what the church does for the individual Christian: Does it encourage him in his faith? Guide him? Provide him with Bible, prayers, hymns, a devotional treasury? Open opportunities for service? Link him with a grand army of believers, global in extent, past and present?

Instances of interdependence may be investigated here. Ask how each person depends on his community (for food, the necessities of life, protection, and common welfare). Why do people flock to cities for a living? What would each person lack if he went it alone—a man without a wife or children without parents, for example? Lead then to a consideration of the interdependence of the believer and his church.

You also may ask what helps people to feel at home in church. Does the church provide this? (Such things may be cited as: a sense of belonging; of being needed; of an opportunity to make a contribution; or of a chance to exercise a special skill for others.)

4. Explore Bible passages.

You will have to be selective in your treatment of passages listed in the pupil's book. Better focus on two or three in some depth than try to cover all. And don't hesitate to inject the study of a passage at some pertinent spot in the session.

The following questions should suggest an approach for dealing with several passages:

Luke 4:15-21   What five purposes are included here? Do they cover all the purposes of the church? Note the mission of Jesus in verses 18-19. The purposes are couched in terms of preaching and social welfare. Can we read into these verses such concerns as education, fellowship, world missions?

John 15:1-16   Where do branches get nourishment? Is it true that the farther a church moves from Christ, the sooner it withers? Did the disciples choose Jesus, or he them—or both? For what purpose?

Ephesians 2:19–22   To what does this passage liken Christ, the apostles, the whole church? Is it farfetched?

Matthew 10:1–4   Why are these men called disciples and apostles? What's the connection between the two terms? The use of a Bible dictionary will be helpful.

Acts 2:44–47   What draws people to a church? Is it the same as we
4:32–35   see in these passages?

5. Have the pupils report on their research project.

Ask for reports pupils have brought on local history. After they cite their information, have them draw conclusions. What do they regard as high points in local church history—the events that evoked greatest sacrifice? Missionary outreach? Is the church most true to its mission when it takes the biggest risks, loses its life for a greater cause?

6. Make assignments for the next session.

Assign the reading of Chapter 3 of the pupil's book, together with Bible passages listed there on a one-a-day plan. Give the class an overview of what to expect in the next session.

A Roving Reporter may be asked to compile information on churches in your area for Session 3. He may also interview young people of other churches on such matters as the vestments of clergy in worship, the layout of their church, the requirements for young people to be received into membership, and any distinctive beliefs these other churches hold.

If you plan to use the research section (7) in Session 3, ask the pupils to procure a list of church councilmen and officers of the congregation. (Church bulletins may provide such a list, though pupils may have to ask older members for names.) A small group of pupils may investigate organizations within the church and prepare a statement about the work and officers of each. This too would require questioning older members, perhaps even the pastor himself.

---

session 3
SCOPE OF SESSION

Your purpose here is to help pupils have a deeper appreciation of their own church—its cardinal practices and emphases. To point up the distinctive features of the Lutheran church you will begin by contrasting the Lutheran church with other churches.

MATERIALS NEEDED

Pupil's book. Bibles. Materials for research project.

Have pencils and paper on hand if you plan to study the church sanctuary.

AN OVERVIEW OF THE SESSION

1. Begin with a report by the roving reporter on his findings about practices and emphases of other churches.

2. Discuss how a newcomer decides which church to attend.

3. Use the Bible passages to see what "personalities" churches can have.

4. Ask what "image" your own church has in the community— how it is regarded and why. Is the image true to the distinctive features of the church?

5. Discuss the three Lutheran emphases examined in the pupil's book. Where are they evident? Do pupils share them?

6. If arrangements permit, move to the church sanctuary to see how the church building can reflect church emphases.

7. Have reports on the research project presented and discussed.

8. Make assignments for the next session.

SESSION PLAN IN GREATER DETAIL

1. Have a report on other churches.

Ask pupils (or the Roving Reporter) to list churches located within a mile or so of your church. Names may be put on a chalkboard. Don't be too concerned about exact distance. Ask pupils what they can report on differences among these churches. What do they know about worship, emphases, where churches got their names? What about ministers' vestments, floor plans of church sanctuaries, their views on dancing and smoking? Even if pupils aren't too accurate in their information, ask for their impressions. When sufficient information has been assembled, ask how serious such differences appear in the eyes of pupils.

2. Discuss which church to attend.

You may ask pupils how they came to attend your church. Friends, proximity, former church affiliation, birth, visiting various churches before deciding—these are the more frequent ways. If any pupil comes from a non-Lutheran background, you may ask his first impressions on attending a Lutheran church and what differences he encountered.

Having discussed the differences among churches, you may ask how we dare regard the church as one. Refer to the Nicene Creed's statement of "One . . . church." Is it so, or is it a dream? Must we all be alike to be one? Or can there be unity in variety? On what essential points are we one (belief in the triune God, in the divinity of Christ, in the church, in our need of salvation)?

If the oneness of the church is apparent, why the differences? Pupils may cite such factors as national backgrounds, different tastes, different personalities who shaped churches, different emphases. Help them feel that, important as these differences are, they dare not obscure the oneness of the church.

3. Explore Bible passages.

This study may be prefaced by a discussion of individualities of churches—the "image" each church seems to have: fashionable, cold, stuffy, self-centered, cliquish, strait-laced. Such traits reflect the distinctive reputation, justified or not, of a congregation. The seven pictures in the Bible passages indicate seven different personalities for early congregations.

To stimulate pointed study ask questions such as:

To which of these early churches would you like to belong?

Is indifference within the church a greater danger than attack from outside?

Can a church's personality and spirit change? How?

With what do we associate early churches in Macedonia, at Philippi, Corinth, Ephesus?

4. Examine the image of your church.

Ask pupils what others say of your church, what impression it makes in the community, what people regard as its strong and weak points. In this discussion it is hoped that the three cardinal emphases (mentioned in Chapter 3 of the pupil's book) will begin to emerge.

5. Relate the three Lutheran emphases to your church.

In discussing the liturgical, educational, and doctrinal emphases, ask where pupils will find them reflected in your own church. Such things as Lenten observance, regard for Good Friday, prominence of the cross reflect our emphasis on the redemptive work of Christ. The *Small Catechism,* extended confirmation instruction, the importance of Sunday church school, parochial schools in some cases, and even theological education reflect our educational emphasis. The pattern of worship and liturgical furnishings suggest the liturgical emphases.

Do pupils regard these as emphases to be treasured and held distinctive of our church? Are they proud of a liturgical church, an educational church, a doctrinal church? Do they regard these as among the contributions of our church to Christendom? Would they cite them as distinctive features to explain why we do what we do in our church?

In this connection, note the frequency of "evangelical" in titles of our churches—a term indicating proclaiming of the gospel.

6. Visit the church sanctuary.

The church sanctuary offers an object lesson on two emphases of our church—liturgical and doctrinal. Let pupils discover signs of these emphases. Colored hangings, names on the hymnboard, and the central position of the altar and pulpit mark the liturgical emphasis. Bibles on the lectern and pulpit, crosses, and the communion rail mark doctrinal emphases.

If time permits, some attention might be given to the floor plan here, with pupils labeling various areas and furnishings in the church.

7. Hear reports and discuss research projects.

Reports by pupils on church personnel and organizations may be presented. Ask how many leaders they can identify by face, as well as by name. Ask about the duties of various officers, the purposes and activities of various organizations.

The unit project is designed to acquaint pupils in an accumulative way with the local congregation. If a manual or newspaper is projected (see the unit introduction), pupils should be selected for this purpose—both to edit material and to assemble further needed information. (If previous classes have prepared a manual, the pupils could bring the existing manual up to date.)

8. Make assignments for the next session.

Assign the reading of Chapter 4 and the Bible passages for the next session. Ask various pupils to carry out research projects such as: drawing a floor plan of the church; locating various articles of furnishing; listing symbols appearing in the church; writing down a brief explanation of symbols. All pupils may engage in the floor-plan project, though some may wish to make the drawing according to scale and in greater detail. The symbol project may be done by a group of pupils; it need not be extensive. Symbols will come under close scrutiny in a future unit.

Ask other pupils to investigate the financial structure of the church. Stewardship materials prepared by the congregation will probably show how offerings are used and include a breakdown of local needs and the needs of the wider church. The church budget also may be used as source material. Local needs should be divided according to areas of work, such as "Ministry of Word and Sacrament," "Music," "Church Property," "Promotion and Administration," and "Debt Service." The wider work might be divided between "Synod and Lutheran Church in America" and "Special Benevolence Causes." Pupils may interview church councilmen for information.

Investigation of the wider work of the church should be apportioned to individual pupils or groups of pupils, each making a study of a separate area. Such reports will cover:

Colleges and seminaries of the Lutheran Church in America: how many; where located; which are supported directly and regularly by local congregation?

Inner-mission agencies and institutions, with special reference to nearby agencies and those supported directly by congregation.

World mission fields — both those supported by the Lutheran Church in America and those by the Lutheran World Federation. Maps will be helpful to show location of fields when making a class report.

Home mission fields, with special reference to procedures for establishing new churches, location of nearby mission churches, and urban work.

session 4

SCOPE OF SESSION

Your purpose here will be to help the pupil feel more at home in public worship, mainly through greater familiarity with the *Service Book and Hymnal* and with the Christian year. More detailed study of worship will come in the next term.

MATERIALS NEEDED

Copies of the *Service Book and Hymnal* (or the book used for worship in your church). Chart of the church year (in the pupil's book). Paper and pencils. Bibles.

AN OVERVIEW OF THE SESSION

1. Discuss the pupils' familiarity with The Service.
2. Examine details of the Service Book and Hymnal.
3. Give an exercise in the Service Book and Hymnal.
4. Study The Service and the church year.
5. Ask pupils to locate Bible passages in The Service.
6. Have reports on the research project. (If you plan an extra session for this unit, make the reports preliminary, with further consideration arranged for the next session. If you have no extra session, merely receive the report, asking that pupils investigate further on their own.)
7. Make assignments for the next session.

SESSION PLAN IN GREATER DETAIL

1. Discuss the pupils' familiarity with The Service.

Ask if pupils can trace the progress and parts of The Service in the *Service Book and Hymnal.* Can they find the proper pages? How much do they know by heart? What gives them the greatest difficulty? List pupils' chief difficulties. An examination of the structure of the book of worship should prove helpful in clearing up their problems.

2. Examine details of the "Service Book and Hymnal."

Distribute copies of the *Service Book and Hymnal.* Have pupils note the following:

a) the binding of two books in a single cover. In some churches hymnals are separate from books of worship. Hymn 1 is the dividing line in our book.

b) the three printings of the same service. Note the printing without music first (the only place for the full text of the Nicene Creed and Prayer of the Church). For worshipers who don't need the music, this word text is sufficient. The two musical settings offer each congregation a choice. Note which setting is used in your congregation.

c) the list of propers for various Sundays and festivals, beginning on page 75. Take an example (say, the twentieth Sunday after Trinity) and ask pupils to insert the correct propers into the framework of The Service. At what point do the introit, collect, and others come?

d) the absence of printed Scripture lessons. Reference may be made to lectionaries here. If you have a copy on hand, show it; if not, explain that a lectionary is a small book with the Bible passages printed in full. Some people like to follow the reading of the lessons in their own books.

e) the location of such sections as Matins, Vespers, the Psalms, special collects, special services, and the General Rubrics. The latter section, with its instructions, may prove especially interesting to pupils.

f) the calendar on pages xi-xii and the section on pages 277–279 dealing with the church year. In studying the pattern of the church year, books should be open to these pages.

3. Give an exercise in the "Service Book and Hymnal."

To make sure pupils can handle the book easily, ask them to indicate pages needed for a service on such days as the second Sunday in Advent, Christmas Eve, Pentecost, Reformation.

4. Study The Service and the church year.

Chapter 4 of the pupil's book may be considered here. Underscore the pattern of The Service, the distinction between fixed and variable elements of worship, and the structure of the church year.

Since The Service will be studied in greater detail in the next term, your purpose here is to provide an overview. The study of Isaiah 6:1–8 may therefore be quite limited. Merely point out the sequence of (*a*) vision, in verses 2–4; (*b*) confession of unworthiness, in verse 5; (*c*) assurance of pardon, in verse 7; (*d*) offering of self, in verse 8.

Ask pupils to examine the chief headings in The Service. Ask if they detect any progress or sense in these parts. Then have them examine Isaiah 6:1–8 for a biblical pattern, and compare the two. Or, ask what they would do if they came together for worship, listing various activities and trying to put them together in some sequence. Have them note throughout the interplay of God's speaking and our responding.

The church year provides your chief laboratory study in this session. Using the chart in the pupil's book and the Calendar and tables of movable dates in the *Service Book and Hymnal,* map the course of the Christian year on a chalkboard. Note:

a) the two halves of the church year, one dealing with our Lord's life, the other with his teaching.

b) the progression of events in the first half, using the Gospels as the basis of study. They begin with announcements of his coming, his birth, his childhood, his public ministry, and lead into his sufferings, death, resurrection, and ascension. Refer to events listed in the Second Article of the Creed.

c) the two elastic seasons of Epiphany and Trinity. The date of Easter determines the length of each. Tables for the Easter date may be used to illustrate this. Point out that this is the one place where the moon governs the church calendar.

d) the significant pivots in the church year. Christmas is always December 25, Epiphany always January 6, Easter the first Sunday after the first moon of spring, and Pentecost seven weeks after Easter. Around these four chart the year on the chalkboard. It will show four Sundays of preparation for Christmas (Advent); Easter, preceded by one forty-day period (Lent) and followed by another (the Easter season); the Trinity season, stretching from Pentecost to a new church year.

e) the chief festivals not included in the Sunday or special schedule above. These will include Reformation Day and saints' days, such as are indicated on pages xi-xii of the *Service Book and Hymnal*. Note the fixed dates and also the limiting of saints' days primarily to apostles and evangelists.

Following your charting of the church year, ask pupils to chart for years when Easter comes on, say, March 25, April 2, or April 16. How many Sundays will Epiphany have? The Trinity season? Can they chart the year with a calendar showing only moon phases?

Some discussion can follow on the value of a church year. Should secular holidays be included or permitted? Does a set series of Bible lessons tend to grow monotonous?

5. Examine the Bible passages.

These passages are all quoted in The Service; the last two occur in the Communion. Pupils should have no trouble recognizing them. As they locate the proper place, you may indicate how much of our liturgy is couched in biblical language without our knowing it.

6. Hear reports on research projects.

Have the pupils report on their projects. Those who have been working on floor plans may show their sketches. Some discussion of terms may be helpful—such as narthex, chancel, nave, lectern, alms basin, retable. Pupils may be interested in comparing these terms with terms used for similar furnishings or areas in public buildings.

Some pupils may have been working on symbols in the church. Let them make their reports, noting the number, variety, and meaning of symbols.

If time permits ask for reports on finances and the church at large. What have pupils (or the Roving Reporter) discovered about financial needs and resources of the church? Try to put down various items in functional form (e.g., instead of "salaries," indicate "ministry of Word," "music," or "property"). If you plan an additional session, you may want to invite a church councilman to discuss the financial picture. The pupils need to be sufficiently introduced to the area that they can ask meaningful questions.

7. Make assignments for the next session.

Unless you plan to use the additional session for this unit, assign the reading of Chapter 5 in the pupil's book and the accompanying Bible passages.

Assign certain pupils to look up in an encyclopedia groups such as Communists, Republicans, Democrats, Boy Scouts, or Camp Fire Girls to see what their underlying beliefs are. Encyclopedia information will be sufficient.

---

an additional session
for unit a (optional)

SCOPE OF SESSION

This session is offered only for classes that plan to have more than thirty sessions in the course. If you haven't done your counting already, do it now, and avoid having to telescope important studies later on.

Admittedly, more is suggested within this unit than can be covered. You're bound to feel somewhat disappointed, partly for having to skim or omit important and interesting studies, partly because these studies appeal to pupils and you want to maintain their interest. But you can't cover everything.

This session may be used to complete work initiated in the unit. No parallel chapter will be found in the pupil's book. Research projects can be pursued during much of the session, with special consideration given to the wider work of the church.

MATERIALS NEEDED

Brochures and leaflets made available to pupils for research during the unit—especially on various causes of the church. Paper and pencils.

AN OVERVIEW OF THE SESSION

1. Continue the exploration of local church finances.
2. Receive reports on the wider work of the church and discuss pupils' findings. Make final plans for putting research findings into manual or newspaper form.
3. Have a summary discussion of the unit.
4. Explore Bible passages, tying review in with the previous study of worship.
5. Preview coming units dealing with matters of personal faith— what it means to believe, why we have creeds, what we mean by believing in God as Father.

SESSION PLAN IN GREATER DETAIL

1. Study church finances.

If arrangements have been made for a councilman to be present, ask him to present salient facts of offerings and disbursements; request that he open the floor to questions. Local needs can be considered here, with a final consideration of wider needs—bridging the path to reports on wider work.

2. Hear reports on the wider work of the church.

Have pupils make their reports. If a lay teacher guides this session, he may want to quiz the pastor in advance or secure materials on: countries in which we engage in mission work through the Lutheran Church in America and the Lutheran World Federation; nearest home mission fields; colleges and seminaries supported by the synod; inner-mission agencies and their work; and causes aided through Lutheran World Action.

3. Have a summary discussion.

Use topics of previous sessions and the pupil's book as a guide. Do pupils understand worship better? Do they feel more at home in the life of the church? Do they know what's expected of them?

Give pupils pencils and paper and ask them to write a few sentences which will complete the following statements:

a) Suppose someone asked you, "Why do we need churches anyway? What is the church for?" What would you tell him? Begin your answer with these words: "The purpose of the church is . . ."

b) Suppose that this same person then said, "O.K., but what can you do about that?" What would you answer? Begin your answer with these words, "I help the church achieve its purpose when I . . ."

4. Explore Bible passages.

Since the Bible passages for this additional session are not printed in the pupil's book, you may list them on a chalkboard, asking pupils to look them up, to arrange them in some kind of sequence, and to see if they can identify them with parts of worship. They are:

a) Matthew 21:1–9 Triumphal entry.
b) John 13:1–15 Upper Room.
c) Luke 2:41–52 Bar Mitzvah.
d) Matthew 4:1–11 Temptation.
e) John 20:19–31 Doubting Thomas.
f) Luke 2:1–4 Song of angels.
g) John 2:1-11 Wedding wine.

These are all lessons appointed for days of the church year. Pupils may arrange them in two ways:

1) in an orderly sequence of events in Jesus' life. The proper sequence would be: *f-c-d-g-a-b-e.*

2) by linking them with days of the church year. A lectionary or copy of the *Service Book and Hymnal* should be used. They are appointed in order for (1) first Sunday in Advent and Palm Sunday, (2) Holy Thursday, (3) first Sunday after the Epiphany, (4) first Sunday in Lent, (5) first Sunday after Christmas, (6) Christmas, and (7) second Sunday after the Epiphany.

5. Preview coming units.

Brief attention may be given here to "where we stand." Having engaged in a preview of the church, its worship and what it expects of us, we move into matters of faith. Note again the profession of faith made at confirmation, underscoring the "I believe."

UNIT B:
beliefs that matter

UNIT OBJECTIVES

1. To help the pupil appreciate the link between belief and conduct.

2. To help him deepen his understanding of faith.

3. To help him discover ways by which God reveals himself, especially through scriptural revelation.

4. To help him appreciate the place and relevance of creeds.

5. To help him begin to formulate his own beliefs.

SCOPE OF UNIT

This unit is preparatory to the detailed study of the articles of the Apostles' Creed. It deals with such topics as the importance of creedal statements, how creeds are formed, what it means to believe, and the place of God's revelation of himself in our belief in God.

Creeds tend to have a formal, rigid sound. Behind these sessions lies an aim to free them of their rigidity. Creeds might be thought of as "principles for living" or a "philosophy of life" that relate men to God.

As in Unit A, the span of sessions is elastic. For a thirty-session year, hold to three sessions. For a longer year, use the additional session (which follows Session 6) and expand the unit to four sessions.

A warning might be given here, lest you be unprepared for a minor letdown in pupil interest. The novelty of the course begins to wear off at this point as pupils shift from the opening sprint into the long pull over the middle stretch. Moreover, it's hard to exceed the study of worship and the church year for sheer fascination; and whatever follows is almost bound to suffer in appeal. And further—you now move from very practical matters into the somewhat "theoretical," from objects to ideas. In short, don't be alarmed if Unit B fails to rival Unit A in interest and attention. (Having been warned, however, keep it to yourself and don't look for special signs of a letdown.)

STRUCTURE OF THE UNIT

No hard and fast limits are set here, so long as you compress the study into the allotted period. You are free to interchange the sessions; they do not observe a necessary progression.

A check test on "What Do You Really Believe?" should introduce this unit and will be useful throughout the unit. It will be helpful in the class's formulation of a creed and will be used again to see if pupils have revised their thinking at the end of the unit.

Study of Bible passages is stressed more than in the previous unit. Since these passages bear so specifically on issues for discussion, Bible study should come early in the session plan.

MATERIALS NEEDED

Book of Concord. Texts of the Apostles' and Nicene Creeds (in the *Service Book and Hymnal*). Bibles for all sessions.

CLASS CREED

The formulation of a class creed is suggested for this unit. Use a part of each session for this purpose rather than trying to complete the assignment in one session.

Formulation of a class creed may appear to be a forbidding assignment for pupils, since they aren't too articulate about their beliefs and will have trouble putting their beliefs into systematic form. However, the importance of this project can scarcely be overestimated. Although pupils will have to struggle to do it and you may feel like throwing in the towel, bear in mind that any effort on this project is success, and that you're dealing with seventh-grade pupils, not theological students. Here are some pointers to help you:

1. The class might be divided into small groups, each group choosing a leader and a recorder. The groups will try to state what they believe about God, about Jesus, about human nature, and about the church. They should as far as possible avoid language used in the Apostles' Creed.

2. The check test "What Do You Really Believe?" can be used as a springboard for each group's discussion. The leader will ask how other pupils feel about statements made there. If they disagree, why? What statement would they substitute? If they find a statement partly true, what does it need to be altogether true? The recorder will keep track of conclusions (on a chalkboard if feasible) and later make a group report to the whole class. For the first session, groups should confine themselves to beliefs in and about God, reserving other sessions for other areas of belief.

3. If more is needed to bring out pupils' beliefs, leaders can be armed with questions, such as:

On belief in God:

> *Is there a God? One or many? How do we know?*
> *What sources of information do we have about him?*
> *What are the characteristics of God? What is he like?*

On belief in Jesus:

> *How do we know anything about him?*
> *What was and is his connection with God?*
> *What did he do? Which events in his life are most important?*
> *By what second name is he best known?*

On belief in human nature:

> *In what ways are men different from animals?*
> *Are we here merely to be born, to live, to die?*

By what standard is human life to be measured?
*Is there any real evidence for life beyond death? What authority
do we have for belief in eternal life?*
On belief in the church:
What keeps the church going?
*What is the church's real purpose? Has it fulfilled this purpose?
What connection does the church have with Jesus?*

4. Pupils will become aware of the purposes behind this class creed as the project develops. These purposes are:

a.) To show how beliefs grow out of experience and are tested and deepened by experience. Don't expect pupils to feel as deeply about some beliefs as you do. They haven't had your experience.

b.) To show how belief in God is focal. What pupils believe about God will soon show up in what they believe about Jesus and human nature. As their creedal statement develops, you may refer pupils back to their previous statement about God.

c.) To show how the creeds of the church emerged. Some of today's issues may be more burning than issues of ancient times; but the issues help determine the inclusion of statements of faith.

d.) To show the necessity of seeking an authority. Pupils will gradually be thrown back on Scripture, on the revelation in Jesus, on the experience and witness of the church. Some basis for testing must be found and agreed on.

e.) To show how weight is given to beliefs most subject to attack. A belief in opposition to communism, for example, will generate more feeling than a belief universally accepted.

f.) To show the need for a positive statement. Creeds are never negative, even though they may imply an opposing point of view.

Pupils should begin to see the process behind the formation of creeds of the church. If the appeal seems strong enough, the small groups may imagine themselves part of the Council of Nicaea, attempting to mold a statement based on Scripture and the witness of the Holy Spirit through the church. You will need to sketch in the dramatic background of the Council of Nicaea and communicate some of the excitement of the occasion if the pupils are to be motivated to use this approach.

5. If the entire class is not too large (not more than twelve to fifteen pupils), you may prefer to make this a class project without division into smaller groups. You can be leader. A recorder will still be needed to indicate points of strong feeling and record class conclusions.

6. Your leadership will be needed more in initiating the project, getting each group off on the right foot, and assembling findings, rather than in actually conducting the groups. A time limit should be placed in advance—perhaps twenty minutes—with additional time provided for assembling the findings at each session. By the unit's close, a complete class creed should be in full view.

OTHER RESEARCH AREAS

Here are some suggested assignments for investigation between class sessions. You may want to ask for individuals or small groups to volunteer for these assignments at the end of Sessions 4 and 5, indicating when reports should be ready. They include:

1. Investigating the underlying beliefs of Communists, Boy Scouts, Republicans, and Democrats (Session 5).

2. Investigating the background of the Apostles' and Nicene Creeds for the additional session. Encyclopedias or books on church history should suffice here.

CHECK TEST

The check test "What Do You Really Believe?" is part of Chapter 5 of the pupil's book. It includes statements that are moderately or widely held today. In no case is any statement entirely satisfactory to a Christian. This is deliberate, in hopes that pupils will want to counter the statement and muster a belief to oppose it.

Allow about ten minutes for the pupils to take the test and share their reactions. Let them feel that it is an opinion poll. Encourage them to put down honestly what they think even if they suspect that what they think isn't what you or the church thinks. By no means assert right answers to show up their wrong ones. Show them you respect their opinions. Keep the matter open-ended. Examine their answers carefully without passing judgment. You will gain many insights into their needs. You will also develop a keen awareness of the direction your teaching should take for each pupil.

For a Christian, statements 11, 12, and 20 will be PT, partly true. It could be argued that statements 13, 15, and 16 are also partly true. With other statements, a Christian would disagree. Much, of course, depends on what the pupils read into the statements.

---

session 5
SCOPE OF SESSION

Throughout this unit you will help the pupil feel the punch and substance in the words "I believe." You will also help him begin to spell out what he believes. The union of belief and conduct, of belief and attitudes, is the core of this session.

MATERIALS NEEDED

The check test "What Do You Really Believe?" (pupil's book, Chapter 5). Bibles. Paper and pencils.

AN OVERVIEW OF THE SESSION

1. Discuss the effect of beliefs on conduct, using Chapter 5 of the pupil's book as a basis. Omit the check test at this point.

2. Ask for reports on beliefs behind Boy Scouts, communism, etc. Cite a few hypothetical cases, asking pupils what code of living would be involved.

3. Explore the Bible passages to examine their "codes for living" (either spelled out or implied) and the effect the codes would have on attitudes and conduct.

4. Ask pupils to check their reactions to statements in the check test "What Do You Really Believe?"

5. Begin the research project on a class creed. Outline procedures to be followed, groups to be formed. Appoint leaders and recorders for various groups. Ask that each group begin by reacting to statements in the check test section "On Belief in God." Collate the findings of the various groups. If little progress has been made in this session, set their hopes for getting order out of chaos on the next try.

6. Make assignments for the next session.

SESSION PLAN IN GREATER DETAIL

1. Discuss Chapter 5 of the pupil's book.

Chapter 5 has a twofold theme: (*a*) the link of belief with conduct and (*b*) the distinction between belief and conviction. The reading of this chapter in the pupil's book should be sufficient to elicit discussion of the first theme. However, you may ask if a motive always lies behind an action, if we always have a reason for doing what we do. Pupils may cite impulsive actions, or those seemingly done without rhyme or reason. Allow for such exceptions. You are trying to stir their thinking here, to help them see the link between belief and action.

The relationship between belief and conviction may require further explanation, since the two words are often used interchangeably. Here a conviction is viewed as a belief that has been fought through—something that can't be taken away. A martyr dies for a conviction. Where a man will "believe" something on the say-so of others, it takes honest doubt and personal struggle to reach a conviction. This may be a pertinent spot to help pupils regard honest doubt not as devilish, but as serving a high purpose.

Also in connection with Chapter 5, you may deal with commitment. We're not concerned with "believing" certain facts about Jesus, but with a personal response to him. Knowing facts about God is one thing; being a believer is something quite different.

2. Hear pupil's reports and examine hypothetical cases.

The first project under "Other Research Areas" (in the unit introduction) should be reported here. If you did not assign the project, outline in brief form the basic tenets of several groups or movements, allowing pupils to fill in with such information as they may have. As each movement is outlined, ask pupils to trace the path from "idea" to "action." What conduct would they expect of a person who believed that way?

Encourage pupils to voice their opinions, whether you agree or not. Here again you're trying to chart the cause-and-effect chain of belief and conduct. Refer again to Chapter 5 of the pupil's book to see how movements such as communism illustrate the very points of that chapter.

If you feel that pupils have grasped this link, you may move to the Bible passages. However, certain hypothetical cases might be marshaled to add further weight. Here you may ask pupils to do some supposing. Suppose they found a twenty-dollar bill in front of their home. What would they do? Suppose they saw an accident at an intersection. What would they do? Suppose they were asked for an answer on a test. Would they pass it on or not? Do not phrase the situations you select in such a way that you telegraph the answers you desire. Make the pupils think! Help them see how their "code for living" shows up in specific situations.

You might assemble codes people live by, do business by, or play games by. To give pupils a start in listing them, you might suggest such codes as: "Win at all costs." "A friend in need is a friend indeed." "Do just enough to get by." "Anything goes, so long as you aren't caught."

After eight or ten codes are listed, ask how people who held such codes would react to the hypothetical situations posed above.

3. Explore Bible passages.

Titles of the passages tend to give the code away. You might ask which codes the pupils regard as worthy of a Christian. Which would tally with the following?

It's nobody's business but my own. (Genesis 4:1–9)
No one is going to look out for you. (Judges 21:25)
Treat other people as you would like them to treat you. (Matthew 7:12)
You can't take it with you, but it's nice to have here. (Mark 10:17–22)

Attention may also be given to courage in believing. Belief is more than accepting facts. It must involve the believer in some kind of personal commitment. You may draw a distinction between knowing facts about Jesus and becoming personally involved in who he was and what he did—or, knowing facts about God and having our feelings, attitudes, and codes shaped by him.

4. Have pupils do the check test.

You could ask the pupils to put their answers to "What Do You Really Believe?" on a separate piece of paper. After the pupils have recorded their opinions one pupil may be asked to summarize the class opinion, showing how the group as a whole feels on these statements. Be sure to collect these answer sheets for use again in Session 7.

5. Begin work on a class creed.

When the class is beginning this project, you may want to keep the whole group together and serve as leader yourself. Have pupils take one or two statements from the check test as a starting point. Ask pupils how they know, how they can be sure. If they claim that God *isn't* an impersonal force, how else would they describe him and why.

If small groups are to be formed, six pupils will be about right for group size. Use your judgment on composition of the various groups—counting off, drawing numbered slips of paper, or grouping bosom pals, if that seems best. Ask each group to deal at this session with belief in God and work toward a statement of what the group believes. If they make little progress, at least the project will be launched for coming sessions. A degree of confusion is to be expected at first.

6. Make assignments for the next session.

Assign the reading of Chapter 6 in the pupil's book. Ask the pupils to think carefully about the various meanings of faith.

session 6
SCOPE OF SESSION

Your central aim here is to help pupils understand what faith is—a relationship of obedient trust between a believer and God. Help pupils feel that faith is their response to God's grace and faithfulness. The word "trust" may be used as a synonym.

You may want to allow more time for the research project and less for discussion in this session. If there is excess time, you may incorporate some of the material from the additional session in this unit.

MATERIALS NEEDED

Pupil's book (Chapter 6). Bibles. Chalkboard. Pencils and paper.

AN OVERVIEW OF THE SESSION

1. *Discuss various instances of "good faith" among persons.*
2. *Explore Bible passages to form an idea of the uses of "faith" in Scripture.*
3. *Discuss the various meanings of faith cited in the pupil's book.*
4. *Continue the research project.*
5. *Make assignments for the next session.*

SESSION PLAN IN GREATER DETAIL

1. Discuss instances of "good faith."

Have the pupils list instances of good faith among persons, e.g.: a paperboy leaving papers with no guarantee of payment later; a variety store putting goods within hand's reach. In some business transactions a handshake seals a bargain; in other, contracts must be drawn up by lawyers. Why? Help pupils feel the importance of trustworthiness as the basis of faith among people. Can most people be trusted? Is it foolish to trust before you suspect?

When the moment seems opportune, you might clinch this by reference to God's faithfulness despite our broken promises. Refer to the Bible passages as a few instances of God's keeping his promise (also other Bible events, for instance, God's rescue of the Israelites or his sending of leaders). Cite these as typical examples of a faithfulness still continued.

2. Explore the Bible.

Ask pupils to find out what the Bible says about faith. List on the chalkboard such possible answers as:

a) *Believing what you know to be untrue.*
b) *Believing what you can't prove.*
c) *Keeping a stiff upper lip.*
d) *Accepting things on the say-so of others.*
e) *Accepting a body of beliefs adopted by the church.*
f) *Trusting and obeying.*
g) *Believing what is highly probable.*

Four of these statements may be inferred from the Bible passages (*b, d, f, g*). Pupils may suggest other statements (for instance Hebrews 11:1), as a definition, or "believing because God is faithful and trustworthy," or "seeing is believing." (Could the reverse be true, that "believing is seeing"?) It is hoped that pupils will find statement *f* the best of the group.

The passages themselves are self-explanatory. Pupils may be asked to review outstanding events of Abraham's life, especially those that exemplify almost blind obedience (e.g., sacrifice of Isaac). They may also examine the passages to see how "obedience" and "probability" seem to clash (e.g., moving mountains, storm at sea). Since the pupil's book brings such points into sharper focus, return to them after studying Chapter 6.

3. Discuss the meanings of faith given in the pupil's book.

A number of commonly held meanings are examined in Chapter 6. Ask pupils if they can offer instances of any of these meanings. If they suggest what faith *does*, ask if it is really faith that does it—or the object of faith. Did a paralytic's *faith* make him whole? Or did Jesus? (Both are correct, as both are needed. The purpose here is to help the pupil feel the importance of faith's object.)

In this connection you might point out the distinction between saying "I believe about God" and "I believe in God." The former doesn't involve the believer at all. Faith involves making a move, committing oneself, taking the leap on the invitation of one who is trusted.

The sections entitled "Faith as Relationship" and "Faith as Obedience" should come in for special discussion. Here you may stress that Christianity is not a set of teachings or an "ism," but a relationship of love and trust. Thus, faith is not in an object, but in a Person. For example, draw the difference between having faith that a chair will support you and having faith in a parent.

The idea of the "degree of probability" may seem over the heads of pupils at first. You may cite instances where it occurs in everyday living—like planning for a party, for Christmas, for any future event. One can be *fairly sure* that the event will come off, or regard it as *highly probable;* but at worst it's merely a calculated risk. However, this is not the same as faith in Christ, or faith as a "daring venture" that obeys despite a low degree of probability.

4. Continue work on a class creed.

If groups are still at work on a statement of belief in God, let them continue. Move on to belief in Jesus when their initial statement is completed.

If you're having trouble getting the project off the ground, don't give up. It's too important for that. Come at it as though no statement of faith had even been formulated. To elicit some provisional statements from pupils, raise basic questions such as: Do you believe there is a God? What is God like? Should we refer to God as "He" or "It"? To be worthy of worship, what must he be? (Bigger than we are? Able to control things we can't control?) Every now and then ask pupils to back up their statements with some evidence.

If your group is small enough to be managed easily, continue the project as a single class group. If smaller groups are more workable, have them continue the initial discussion in smaller units. Ask for a summary statement after a reasonable length of time.

5. Make assignments for the next session.

Assign Chapter 7 in the pupil's book for study. (If you plan to use the additional session ask the pupils to reread Chapter 6 and to look up articles on the Apostles' and Nicene Creeds in encyclopedias.)

---

an additional session
for unit b (optional)

SCOPE OF SESSION

This session bears on the sections of Chapter 6 of the pupil's book dealing with the creeds of the church: how they came to be; what they include, how they are used today; why we retain ancient words. Such a study will provide background for the next unit on the

First Article of the Creed, and also lay the groundwork for the creedal studies of the coming two years.

MATERIALS NEEDED

Hymnals or service books containing the Nicene Creed for each pupil. A dictionary. Bibles. Chalkboard. Pupil's book (Chapter 6). A copy of the *Book of Concord*.

AN OVERVIEW OF THE SESSION

The final three sections of Chapter 6 of the pupil's book provide a framework for this session. Using it as a guide:

1. Discuss the over-all purpose of creeds.
2. Consider the background of the general creeds, comparing the Apostles' and Nicene Creeds, discussing the origin of both, reading samples from the Athanasian Creed.
3. Explore certain Bible passages to look for creedal statements.
4. Ask pupils what terms in the Apostles' and Nicene Creeds they do not understand, and discuss substitute words.
5. Work on the class creed.
6. Make assignments for the next session.

SESSION PLAN IN GREATER DETAIL

1. Discuss the purpose of creeds.

Emphasize that a creed is an historic statement, based on issues in controversy at the time of formulation. Ask, for example, why major sections of Jesus' life are omitted. (Because they were generally accepted; no one challenged them.)

Ask how creeds are used today. (As historic statements of faith, as forms by which Christians today confess their faith, as guidance for faith.)

Pupils may have an impression that the creeds deal with God, Jesus, and the Holy Spirit (as though the first part dealt with God alone, and not with God as Father). Note here that the entire creed deals with belief in God, and that a Christian's view of God is through Jesus Christ. Even God the Creator is thus viewed through Christ; and so is God's work in nature. This is a basic point of view that will merit emphasis throughout the whole course. Relate this emphasis to the formulation of the class creed.

2. Examine the background of general creeds.

If you assigned them, this would be the spot for reports on a comparison of Apostles' and Nicene Creeds and on the origins of both creeds (see the unit introduction). If no such assignments were made, you yourself may want to report briefly on the origins (using a church history as your source). The entire group can examine the two creeds, noting points of difference, especially in the Second and Third Articles. Ask pupils why there should be such a difference, whether the two statements are in disagreement, and whether one elaborates on the other.

Your point here is to help pupils see how each creed came out of its own historical setting (attacks on the divinity of Christ were sharper when the Nicene Creed was forged, for example).

Introduce pupils briefly to the Athanasian Creed (use the *Book of Concord*) here, noting how it deals with inter-relationships of the Persons of the Trinity. Direct your remarks mainly to answering the question "Who was Jesus?" Read some sample statements from the Creed and show pupils its length to explain why it is not better known and used in the church.

3. Explore Bible passages.

The seven passages listed here are not given in the pupil's book. You may write all seven on the chalkboard, but limit your study to those that can be explored within your time limits.

Acts 10:34–43 Jesus is Lord.   *Acts 13:26–31 Crucified and raised.*
1 Corinthians 15:3–7 Easter   *2 Timothy 2:8–9 Remember Jesus*
facts.   *Christ.*
Acts 4:18–20 Urge to speak.   *Ephesians 4:9–10 The descent.*
John 1:1–3, 14 The Word.

Ask pupils to read these passages noting their similarity to statements in the general creeds, and identifying vestigial statements of faith. Ask what facts of Jesus' life are cited, how he is viewed, how early Christians regarded his work. Acts 10 includes the earliest creed, "Jesus is Lord"; 1 Corinthians 15 emphasizes the central position of Christ's resurrection; Ephesians 4 gives the New Testament basis for a phrase in the Apostles' Creed. Have pupils feel that they are tracing the Apostles' Creed back to its pre-creedal origins.

4. Define unfamiliar creedal terms.

Let pupils list on the chalkboard terms that are unfamiliar. The Nicene Creed will have more such terms than the Apostles' Creed. Some terms may baffle you for explanation ("conceived," "begotten," "substance," "very"). Ask for substitute terms or phrases ("came from God" for "conceived" and "begotten"; "identical" for "one substance"; "true" for "very"). If necessary, consult a dictionary. While such substitutes may not be precise, they should suffice for pupils at this point.

5. Continue work on the research project.

Only if you are treating this optional session as a separate session will you continue the research project at this spot. You are moving toward a final stage in this project. Even if the pupils' creedal statement is quite faulty, commend their efforts.

Ask pupils to compare their statement with items of the Apostles' Creed. Have they said much the same thing in different words? Have they left anything out? Is their own statement implied in the Apostles' Creed?

6. Make assignments for the next session.

Assign Chapter 7 in the pupil's book.

session 7
SCOPE OF SESSION

This session deals with authority in religion, especially the authority of the Word in Scripture on matters of faith and life. The pupils' research project should prepare them for this study, since a statement of faith forces them back to some authority—whether their own ideas, their own wishes, what they have heard, or the truths of the Bible.

A cardinal objective is to help pupils view the Scriptures as the faithful record of God's acts through and with his people, acts culminating in the life and work of our Lord. Through these acts, and supremely through Christ, God reveals his will and ways to us.

MATERIALS NEEDED

Pupil's book (Chapter 7 and the check test "What Do You Really Believe?"). Pupils' original answer sheets to the check test. Bibles. Chalkboard. Paper and pencils.

AN OVERVIEW OF THE SESSION

1. Discuss evidence for God's existence.

2. Ask what authority pupils used in arriving at the beliefs stated in the class creed.

3. Consider Chapter 7's emphasis on God's disclosure of himself through words, deeds, and life (the life and work of Christ).

4. Explore the Bible passages with an eye to ways by which God disclosed his will and ways or ways by which men "found" God.

5. Conclude the research project.

6. Complete the check test again, asking pupils to comment on their answers.

7. Make assignments for the next session.

SESSION PLAN IN GREATER DETAIL

1. Discuss evidence for God's existence.

How would pupils answer a person who claims you can't be sure or can't know? A person who doesn't want to believe? Are there any real proofs for God?

You're not trying to marshal arguments here, but simply to set the stage for seeking an authority. Pupils may cite the orderliness of the world, the universality of belief, and the existence of the soul.

You may ask if only seen and felt things are real, or if there is reality in the unseen and intangible. Electricity and the atom are illustrations of unseen realities. Another is pain, which can be proved only to one who wants to believe.

Ask if belief in God hinges on *wanting* to believe, and thereby inventing God. Or does God disclose himself in some way? Pupils with scientific interests can cite their own examples of unanswered questions that suggest God is behind natural forces. The change of matter into energy may be one example, like the burning of a candle where nothing is lost, but where the form is changed. If you are not of a scientific bent yourself, this is where you can become a listener while pupils inform you of unseen things that are real.

2. Probe the authority for our beliefs.

Ask why pupils believe as they do. Why have they written what they have so far in the class creed? What grounds do they have? Who or what gives them the right? Is this authority reliable? How can they decide what authority to follow? How would they determine a reliable authority for such things as playing a game, pronouncing a word, hanging a flag? Is authority in religion determined the same way? Point out that Christianity receives its authority directly from the Word of God which is conveyed through the Bible and is incarnate in Jesus.

If pupils have trouble with the word "authority," use some synonym or phrase, like: How do you know? How can you be sure? What do you have to go by? If you seek the correct pronunciation of a word, you must establish an authority first—say, Webster or Oxford—otherwise the matter remains unsettled.

3. Review the main ideas in Chapter 7 of the pupil's book.

Chapter 7 explains what we mean by the "Word of God." In pupil's language the Word is whatever spoken or unspoken, communicates God's will and ways to us; it is known supremely and measured by God's saving work in Christ. Help pupils feel how this Word can come to us through preaching, teaching, catechism, sacraments, and witness of the church.

The connection of the Word and Scripture deserves consideration. Scripture is God's Word; it records for us God's saving acts, which reach their climax in Christ. You (or pupils) may cite instances to illustrate this: the rescue from Egypt, the raising up of Gideon and Samson, God's speaking through prophets, or any other act that shows God's love for his people. It is this record that gives the Bible its supreme authority. (How else, for instance, would we know anything about Christ's saving work?)

To make this clear to pupils, ask what a word is. Why do we use words? What are they supposed to do? Could the mating song of a bird be called a "word"? Could a frown, a smile, a handshake? Through such questions help pupils understand a "word" as a means of conveying thoughts and feelings—like a bridge between persons. It has to be intelligible, coming as close as language can come to precise communication. But it's more than verbalizing, and this may be a point of confusion for pupils. We're apt to limit it to what can be printed or read or spoken, not realizing that thoughts can be conveyed in other ways. (Often the deeper the feeling, the less we rely on words to express that feeling—as in grief or joy or gratitude, where we resort to unspoken symbols like a hug, a gift, or perhaps tears.)

Such a discussion should help pupils understand how God's revelation can be called his "Word." While the term implies more than communication, this definition at least provides a clue.

4. *Explore Bible passages.*

Three of these passages show God revealed through Christ (John, Matthew, Philippians). 1 Kings 19 contrasts God's speaking through a still small voice with the noise and "big splash" of nature's upheavals. Psalm 139 describes how we are found by God when we are seeking to find him. 2 Peter points up the disclosure of God through a written record and eyewitness; Isaiah 40, through being overwhelmed by our smallness.

Ask pupils if they can think of other passages clearly revealing God (e.g., John 3:16; the crucifixion and resurrection narratives in all four Gospels; Genesis 1; Exodus 20).

5. *Conclude the research project.*

Allow the pupils some time to complete work on the class creed. Ask pupils how they liked the project. Commend those who worked faithfully on it. Recognize the difficulties in trying to phrase a statement of belief, noting that the church itself took centuries to put the two creeds into the form we have today.

6. *Go over the check test again.*

Now is a good time for pupils to take the check test again to see whether their ideas have changed during the past three or four sessions. Return the answer sheets and ask pupils to write their answers again in a second column. They may also write comments about their answers to explain why they agree or disagree with a statement; to explain which part of a "partly true" statement is true and which is false; or to tell why they have changed their original answer. If time permits, discuss their answers.

7. *Make assignments for the next session.*

Ask pupils to read Chapter 8. Request several interested pupils to make a brief report on how science views the origin and development of life.

UNIT C:
God as father

UNIT OBJECTIVES

1. *To help the pupil deepen his sense of wonder before God.*
2. *To assist him in deepening his relationship with God the Father through knowing God as Creator, Provider, and Protector.*
3. *To help him interpret the place of evil in life.*
4. *To help him feel God's purpose for his own life.*

SCOPE OF UNIT

Luther's explanation of the First Article of the Creed provides the focus and content of this unit dealing with God's revelation as Creator, Provider, Protector, and, supremely, as Father. Human nature —the gap between the persons we are and the persons God meant us to be—is seen in the light of this revelation. To review the doctrinal basis, reread the first theological background article.

The relationship of Father and child is basic to these sessions. Some pupils may have negative attitudes toward their parents. You will need warm understanding of their problems in order to help them accept God as their heavenly Father. You are concerned not with proving God or describing him, but with aiding the pupil in strengthening his relationship with God as Father. Out of this relationship comes the Christian view of God's work in creating, providing, protecting, and preserving.

The sessions will cover many important areas of Christian teaching —its view of the world around us, of human sin, of the providence of God. The pupil's book provides a quick summary of areas covered.

STRUCTURE OF THE UNIT

The eight sessions provided for this unit may be adapted to your local situation. Don't force each session of your class to correspond with a session outlined here. Follow the suggestions but keep the unit flowing according to the needs and interests of your pupils. The use of audio-visual aids, for example, would require adjustment of session plans.

The nature of this unit's study reduces the possibilities for motor activities. Bible exploration will provide something of a change of pace, as will pupil reports and audio-visual aids.

RESEARCH AREAS

In this unit, no unit-long projects are suggested. Research projects will be topics or items of investigation for small groups of pupils or individual pupils.

Pupils may be asked to choose from a list of topics or projects placed on the chalkboard the topic or area they would like to investigate.

76

A time schedule for reports should be given at the same time. It would be well to schedule the research projects throughout the unit.

Session 8: (Assigned in Session 7.) How science views the origin and development of life. How the world of nature came to be what it is.

Session 9: Hymns that speak of God's power.

Session 10: Debate on the proposition, "We are to blame for conditions today." (Two pupils for each side.) A report on the Devil in the Bible. (Use a Bible dictionary and concordance.)

Session 11: Report on the United Nations Commission on Human Rights (include statements of the Commission and problems faced). Report on significant milestones in the story of human rights (events and documents such as the Declaration of Independence and the Emancipation Proclamation).

Session 12: Report on news items that tell of conflict of claims on a child's time and loyalty (like the rights of a school or of a family).

Session 13: Debate on the proposition, "Every man is entitled to all he can get, so long as he does it legally." (Two pupils for each side.)

Session 14: Report on careers in the church.

Session 15: Report on what the Gospels tell us of Jesus' teaching about God as Father. (Use one pair of pupils for Matthew-Luke, and another pair for the Gospel of John.)

MATERIALS NEEDED

Materials for research projects should be available to pupils. These include: Bible dictionaries and Bible concordances (several copies that need not be identical); printed leaflets on church careers and stewardship; and copies of the hymnal used in worship. For some research projects (like UN statements), pupils can do their own digging if library facilities are available.

Audio-visual equipment will be needed if films are to be shown. Bibles for all sessions. *Small Catechism* (in pupil's book).

EXPLAINING RESEARCH WORK

Before pupils make their choice, they may ask for an explanation of various research areas—how to go about it, where to find information, what its purpose is. Some help is offered here:

Session 8: Present the case for science—theories advanced in school texts for origins of the universe and of life and for evolution.

Session 9: Read through words of hymns to see which would be fitting. You may cite an example like "For the beauty of the earth" and suggest a limit of eight or ten appropriate hymns.

Session 10: The debate may probe whether parents and society are to blame, or other persons living today; can we pass the buck? Researchers on the Devil should use the Bible dictionary and concordance to look up verses with words such as "Tempter," "Adversary," "Satan," and "Devil" and try to see what they add up to.

Session 11:   Pupils investigating the United Nations may consult school-books or library books, or write to the United Nations for printed information. Reporters on human rights may get help from printed leaflets from the UN and consult library books and encyclopedias. (A project for a sharp pupil!)

Session 12:   A sample case might be a parent's decision to educate his own child at home challenged by the state and school.

Session 13:   The proposition might be restated, "How much responsibility does a man have for what he earns and amasses? Is it all his, or should he share it with others?"

Session 14:   The pastor may help with printed material here, showing the kinds of full-time careers in the church and what is required.

Session 15:   Using a concordance, find references to the word "Father"; examine verses and draw conclusions.

Hymn Detective

Pupils who choose the research for Session 9 may be asked to be "Hymn Detectives" for the entire unit. They will be responsible for choosing hymns (to be said or sung), prayers and worship materials keyed to session themes. They can use the chapters of the pupil's book as their guide. Hymnals and books of worship will be resource material for hymns and prayers.

AUDIO-VISUAL AIDS

Two unit areas—God's created world and Christian vocation—offer a use for audio-visual aids.

The filmstrip *God's Wonderful World* treats several aspects of God as Creator. Topics include the magnitude of creation, its variety, unity and order, and its continuing process. The filmstrip has 69 frames, full color, and two scripts. It is available from the Christian Education Press for $5.50.

Other available audio-visual aids have certain drawbacks. The films *Dust or Destiny* and *Red River of Life* in the Moody Bible Institute's "Sermons from Science Series" would require a bulk of session time and rent for $17.50 or more. They present God's wonderful world in pictorial style, but allow little time or disposition for discussion.

Films and filmstrips on stewardship have a bearing on Christian vocation, though a career emphasis should be sought rather than a monetary theme. A good filmstrip to use is *Christian Commitment* (Family Filmstrips, 43 frames, color, $6.50).

CHECK TEST AND MEMORY WORK

A check test is included in this unit. Ask pupils to check their answers in Session 8 and again in Session 15. This will provide a point of comparison to measure pupils' growth in understanding.

While no provision is made for memory drills in these sessions, it is expected that by the conclusion of the unit pupils will know Luther's explanation of the First Article by heart. A group device that may prove effective is the use of Luther's meaning as a group confession of faith during the period of class worship. Pupils can use their *Small Catechism* to read this confession of faith, though they should be encouraged to use their books less and less for prompting from week to week. The chalkboard may be used instead of the books. Erase portions of Luther's statement from week to week so that the pupils must fill in the missing words for themselves. Don't label this a memorizing device, since you want to encourage the use of Luther's explanation as an act of worship. However, before the unit concludes, ask each pupil to repeat Luther's meaning either privately or at some time in the group session.

---

session 8
SCOPE OF SESSION

In this session you will turn back the clock and deal with origins, contrasting the emphasis of religion to that of science. Three ideas should dominate: (1) God is Creator; (2) his creation is good; and (3) man is the highest of God's creatures. The session will contemplate the wonders of God's created world and then turn to the Bible passages dealing with God's creative work.

MATERIALS NEEDED

Pupil's book, paper and pencils for check test. If a filmstrip is to be shown, you will need projection equipment and the filmstrip itself set up prior to the session. Bibles.

AN OVERVIEW OF THE SESSION

1. Have the pupils take the check test in Chapter 8.
2. Have a general discussion of the wonders of nature, with pupils adding their own observations and examples.
3. Use Chapter 8 of the pupil's book to arouse curiosity about origins of things commonplace today.
4. Have the pupils read Luther's explanation of the First Article of the creed. Note the emphasis on creation "of me."
5. Probe and discuss the Bible passages.
6. Gather the threads of the discussion together, underscoring the three cardinal ideas listed under "Scope of the Session."
7. Make assignments for the next session.

SESSION PLAN IN GREATER DETAIL

1. Begin with the check test (or filmstrip).

Distribute paper and pencils. Allow enough time for pupils to complete the check test in the pupil's book. Do not call it a *check test*. Tell the pupils that this is an opportunity to express what they really believe. You are not after "right" answers at this point. You want to help the pupils see the patterns of their understandings of and attitudes toward God. Collect the answer sheets for use again during the last session of this unit.

If a filmstrip is to be shown, allow some time to discuss its contents and defer the check test to the next session.

2. Discuss the wonders of nature.

The closing section of Chapter 8 of the pupil's book may be used for discussing the wonders of nature. Encourage pupils to try their hand at solving mysteries posed in that section. Your group may thus discuss the mystery of instincts, the ratio between reproduction and chance of survival, the communication system of ants, or the location of a bird's eyes (whether hunter or hunted). Pupils should be encouraged to offer examples of their own. In many instances they will probably enlighten *you* (a role they'll enjoy).

3. Probe the difference between science and religion, creating and making.

The rest of Chapter 8 of the pupil's book comes under discussion here. Several points will emerge in this discussion: (*a*) How "creation" suggests something in the far, dim past. It takes us into the study of origins, largely to see how wheels were once set in motion. (This idea will be counteracted when you deal with Luther's explanation.) (*b*) How religion and science view creation. Science is concerned with natural laws and how they work, arriving at its theories through the study of such laws. Religion comes at it through faith in God as Creator, establishing the laws. Science is interested in the process; religion in the meaning and purpose. (*c*) The distinction between creating and making. Creating begins with nothing and ends with something; making merely changes what is already here.

These emerging points will certainly not be stated in just this way by the pupils. They are meant for your benefit, largely to give direction to the discussion.

A rereading of appropriate sections of the article "God the Father and Creator" in this teaching guide will also provide needed background direction here.

4. Study Luther's explanation.

Set the significance of Luther's explanation of the First Article against this curiosity about origins. Luther barely alludes to it. Instead he deals with the question "Where do I come in?" His emphasis is on God's creative work here and now, not just in some dim past.

5. Explore Bible passages.

Considerable time should be allotted to the Bible passages. At least five of the seven should be studied (you may omit Psalms 104 and 33). You may prefer to reverse the order of passages, saving the two Genesis passages until last. Such a reversal would bring to the fore the poetical descriptions of God's creative work and set the tone for dealing with the Genesis passages. (This reverse order is followed in the comments below.)

The passages from Psalms and Isaiah are hymns to the Creator God. As pupils study them, ask how the world of nature is described, what its purpose is, whether they would agree with these poetic lines. Are poems to be taken literally?

Psalm 19 might be used to help pupils feel the significance of religious truth. Ask pupils how they would describe the sun. A ball of gas? An inferno of heat? What would the sun be to an artist, a tropical native, a farmer, a plant, a poet? Which view is right? (All, in a way!) Is this the sense in which the psalmist pictures the sun—as a sign of God's faithfulness, glory?

The same might be said of the views of the world expressed in Isaiah and Job. Is that the way we describe the world—like curtains stretched from horizon to horizon, or with morning stars singing for joy?

Ask if pupils see any real conflict between science and the Bible in the two Genesis passages. Find out what they are studying in their science classes in school. It will be helpful if you borrow a copy of their textbook and browse through it, paying particular attention to any theories of creation advanced. Do not raise questions about conflicts that do not exist for them. We do not want to spend time answering questions they are not asking yet. Ask the pupils who investigated science's answers to the problems of the origin and development of life to report.

If the pupils are interested, you can deal with questions such as these: Could science provide some answers to the progression, the gradual stages, while religion can provide the answer to Who did the creating? What does Genesis say about the purpose of Creation? About the climax of Creation in man? Are we to think of the origins as though a switch were pulled in an instant? Or can we think of rocks millions of years in forming? *Make the point:* science answers "how"; Christianity answers, "why."

Don't worry if such questions puzzle the pupil. They're meant to. You're helping him go beyond bare fact to think of meaning—to take facts and see what they add up to when related to God. (A similar brain-teaser: take bread and ask what it is—merely so much flour and salt and vitamins? Is that what it is to a starving man? A baker? A communicant? The one definition deals with bare fact, the others with meaning.)

6. Summarize.

After gathering the threads of the discussion together, ask pupils to reread Luther's explanation of the First Article of the Creed. Indicate its emphasis on creating *me*, not merely the origins of life around us. While curiosity about origins is natural and important, the central fact of faith is what the Apostles' Creed means for each person here and now.

7. Make assignments for the next session.

Encourage reading Chapters 8 (again) and 9 in the pupil's book. Check on the research projects to see how they are advancing. If you are planning a debate for the next session, check with the pupils involved to make sure they will be prepared. Check the unit introduction for details.

---

session 9
SCOPE OF SESSION

Whereas the previous session dealt with God as Creator, this one centers on God Almighty. His omnipotence is seen first as raw power and nothing more. Then, against that view of awesome might is thrust the Christian view of the *Father* Almighty, God using his power as a father would—as an instrument of love.

MATERIALS NEEDED

News clippings of violent upheavals of nature (fire, flood, hurricane). Bibles. Pupil's book (Chapter 9).

AN OVERVIEW OF THE SESSION

1. Begin with a discussion of our fear and worship of power.
2. Using Chapter 9 of the pupil's book, ask what God would be like if he were only all-powerful.
3. Discuss the human use of power.
4. Explore the Bible passages with an eye for revelation of God's power and, even more, to see how he uses it.
5. The Hymn Detective can make his report.
6. Make assignments for the next session.

SESSION PLAN IN GREATER DETAIL

1. See the relationship between awe and fear and power.

Begin by asking pupils to describe the biggest display of power they have ever seen. Compare the power of the hydrogen bomb with the power of a tornado or an earthquake. Show them clippings to illustrate. After examples and experiences have been cited, ask what reaction they had to these displays. Fear? Awe?

Discuss the human worship of power. Ask why we boast of the biggest plane, the most powerful motor, the largest building. Is it because we feel so small and want to make ourselves feel big? Is it because we are insecure? What about the motives behind the building of the Tower of Babel (Genesis 11:1–9)?

Will pupils feel that size and success are one and the same? The more men you have under you, the bigger your position! The bigger the corporation, the more successful it must be! Will they regard size as a measure of quality?

2. Focus on God's power.

Ask pupils how they would look on God if he were only all-powerful. Would they fear him? Would he be uncaring, unsparing, much like a violent upheaval of nature that cares nothing about persons? Is this why we have so many superstitions, largely to get on the right side of an angry, uncaring God?

Do good luck charms, rabbit's feet, avoiding walking under ladders, or crossing oneself before shooting a basket fall into this category? How about the American Indians "stepping light because a spirit lurked in every tree"? Or the Africans building low fences around their property to keep the evil spirits away? What kind of God lies behind such beliefs and practices?

Another way to come at the same point is through discussing whether might makes right. Does it seem that way in national affairs (where the mighty nation forces its will on the weaker one)? How about majority rule? Is it always right? (Remember the majority crucified Christ.)

3. Examine men's use of power.

Ask what pupils would do if they had power at their command. (You might get some silly answers here, but pass them by with a quip.) Typical answers might be: wipe out our enemies; get to the top of the heap; amass a fortune. How much of this is wise use of power? How much is selfish? What examples can pupils cite of persons with too much power? How have such persons used or abused it? (Instances might be cited of tyranny, of wiping out rivals, or gaining further power.)

Ask if we can ever trust humans with power. Is it true that "power corrupts, and absolute power corrupts absolutely"? Is it true that those we can trust shrink from power, and those who want it can't be trusted?

Have men ever used their power to benefit mankind? (You might discuss Andrew Carnegie and his establishment of public libraries.) Make a transition from this point to consideration of God using his power to benefit men. His love motivates his power.

4. Explore Bible passages.

If time is limited choose one or two passages instead of trying to deal with all of them. To sharpen the study use such key questions as:

Psalms 93, 97:1-5. How is God's omnipotence described here? Have you ever heard the roar of a flood? Of waves breaking on the shore? What bearing has this on God's power?

Psalms 90:1-6. What evidences of God's power are found here? To what do they point? (His faithfulness?)

Isaiah 40:27-31. To what use does God put his power here (and in the Mark 4 passage)? How does it compare with our own use of power?

Matthew 11:2–6. If God himself were to come to earth, by what signs would we recognize him? Would they be signs of power or of mercy? Does this lie behind John's doubt?

5. Have the Hymn Detective report.

If you are pressed for time, merely receive the pupil's report. Its value is not sufficient to involve the whole group too deeply, especially if it means taking time from other parts of this session. Regard the following suggestions as optional.

Many hymns under "City, Nation, and World" express the thought of God as King of kings and Lord of lords. Hymns of creation are also appropriate here. Pupils may examine hymns themselves, adding their own feeling as to their fitness to express God's omnipotence.

In this connection you may indicate again how the Christian view of God as Father colors the conception of his omnipotence. Because he is Father, his power—to judge and condemn, but also to save—is an agent of love. Pupils should note the sequence in the Creed: "God the *Father* Almighty." A brief rereading of Luther's explanation will suffice to underscore this. Hymns chosen by the Hymn Detective can be examined along this line—to see how God's fatherhood is implied, if not actually expressed. We cringe in fear before raw power; but we find security in friendly power.

6. Make assignments for the next session.

Be sure to check the progress of the research reports you are anticipating for the next session. Assign Chapter 10 and the Bible passages for careful study.

---

session 10
SCOPE OF SESSION

Sessions 10 and 11 turn the spotlight on man. Session 12 deals with man's selfishness and pride; Session 13 with his calling as a child of God. Man's self-centeredness is here viewed as spoiling the world God made. Man wants to be the center of the show; man's self-interest puts him in conflict with others; man wants to play God. You will want to help each pupil see that these basic impulses are a part of his human nature. The Bible passages and pupil's book provide key tools in this study.

MATERIALS NEEDED

Bibles. Pupil's book (Chapter 10).

AN OVERVIEW OF THE SESSION

1. Examine the Bible passages in the light of Chapter 10.
2. Have the research report on the Devil in connection with the Garden of Eden passage.

84

3. *Have a debate.*

4. *Use Luther's explanation of the First Article of the Creed devotionally.*

5. *Make assignments for the next session.*

SESSION PLAN IN GREATER DETAIL

1. Explore Bible passages in the light of Chapter 10.

The Bible passages provide a structure of the themes presented in the pupil's book. Guide the class in discussing the themes as they study these Scripture references.

Begin by asking the pupils how they would improve the world as they find it. What's wrong with it? Did God mean it to be the way it is? What happened to' make it as it is? Move to a discussion of the three Genesis passages. Have one or two pupils read the passages aloud. Ask them if they understand the basic ideas of each passage. Put these ideas on the chalkboard.

Can you help pupils picture the Genesis stories as the story of each person, not merely of those who lived in ancient times? Each person is created in the image of God; each is given dominion and freedom of choice; each soon puts himself at the center of things; each collides with others. The three Genesis stories are therefore illustrative of the repeated history of every individual.

Develop a degree of familiarity with these stories, and help pupils see beyond literal meaning. Let the "fruit" suggest freedom of choice, the "serpent" evil, the struggle of Cain with Abel, jealousy through a collision of interests. Can pupils see repeated instances of these stories?

Discuss the fact that each person begins life helpless. He can't begin where others leave off. He makes the same blunders; needs the same education; begins without teeth or hair and ends the same way. Is this what makes the Gensis story so perpetually up to date? Doesn't every man go through the experience of turning against God?

In connection with Psalm 8, ask if God didn't take a foolish risk in creating man with such power and then giving him freedom to use it as he chose. Would things be better in the world if men were like toys or puppets, controlled by God? If so, why did God take this risk? (The analogy of a father might come into the picture. What kind of a father would want his son to be merely a puppet, despite the risk he confronts in letting him choose for himself?)

Psalms 51:1–12 and 78:32–38 provide an opportunity to describe human sin in terms of broken promises and offenses against God. You may indicate the prodigal's use of Psalm 51 (in Luke 15). Help the pupil understand how each person must measure himself by what God expects of him (in conduct and attitude and especially in relationships of love and faithfulness).

Revelation 21:1–4 provides a view of last things, a kind of return to the Garden of Eden. It foresees God's final triumph despite the selfishness and pride of man.

2. Hear the research report on the Devil.

A discussion can follow the pupil's report on the Devil in the Bible. Questions like these could launch it: Do you believe in the Devil today? How would you describe him? Why do we make him appear like a snake (we don't like crawling things) or dress him in red tights, put a fork on his tail and horns on his head? Would you be attracted to a devil who looks like that? Are we referring to the Devil when we ask, "What ever got into him to do that?" Why is he spoken of as "the prince of this world" or "the great deceiver" in the Gospel of John? Just what is he up to?

Certain guides may be helpful in leading this discussion:

a) The Devil is the personification of evil in the world. (Be careful to keep this point from becoming a vague generality.)

b) Deception—making the bad appear good, the good appear bad, the devilish appear godly—is his stock in trade.

c) He thrives on being undetected and delights in being dismissed as a nonentity.

d) He appeals to man's pride and selfishness.

e) He can be dismissed or disregarded only when evil can be disregarded. (Note the forces unleashed by war and war's backwash as classic instance of the Devil's superhuman power.)

f) In the Old Testament he is chiefly regarded as a tester (as in the story of Job 1).

3. Have a debate.

Following the Bible study, allow time for the debate (with two to three minutes given to each debater). Pupils can follow with their own reactions. If no debate has been planned, let pupils discuss the positive and negative sides of the proposition, "We are to blame for conditions today." The section "If You Were God" in the pupil's book would help in this. In fact, you may find a reading of the entire chapter helpful in a preliminary way. In such a reading, ask pupils to withhold comments until relevant Bible passages come under study.

Indicate in advance that no decision will be made about a winner. Pupils should merely summon reasons for each point of view without getting into petty arguments. Some points that may be made for each side:

The proposition: "We are to blame for conditions today."

Positive: We can't evade our individual responsibility by laying blame entirely on parents and society (Ezekiel 18:1–4 gives an assist on this excuse); we're to blame if we keep the vicious circle of conditions going.

Negative: We inherited things like taxes; conditions we are born into are of others' making; we are like pawns on a board, moved by forces we can't control.

Following the debate, ask whether, if we were to start all over again, the world would be better? How soon would it fall back to where it is? What's responsible for this weakness? This closing discussion will bring you full circle to the "image of God" and the Garden of Eden.

4. *Use Luther's explanation of the First Article of the Creed devotionally.*

Have the group read the words together and then join in the Lord's Prayer.

5. *Make assignments for the next session.*

Assign Chapter 11 in the pupil's book. Check with pupils doing research on human rights projects due at the next session.

---

session 11

SCOPE OF SESSION

Session 10 dealt with man created in the image of God. Man marred that image through pride and selfishness. In this session we help the pupil see man as a child of God, precious to God despite his sinfulness. The emphasis is on the worth of man—not because of his intrinsic value, but because of God's love.

MATERIALS NEEDED

Service Book and Hymnal. Bibles. Pupil's book (Chapter 11). Some personal trinkets: a souvenir, a keepsake, or an old photograph.

AN OVERVIEW OF THE SESSION

1. Begin by showing the pupils a trinket and asking them to appraise its value. What basis do they use for deciding its worth?
2. Discuss various values of a man.
3. Ask how man can be valued more highly by God than by other men. If God sets an impossible standard before us, how can we be worth so much to him?
4. Explore Bible passages to examine God's appraisal of man.
5. Use the confessional section of The Service for its emphasis on man as a sinner and yet as a child of God.
6. Move to some implications of this in terms of human rights. Ask for research reports.
7. Summarize by a statement the idea that our worth tells us more about God's love than about ourselves. Indicate what happens when we look on people as things, not as persons.
8. Make assignments for the next session.

SESSION PLAN IN GREATER DETAIL

1. Appraise the value of a trinket.

Lead pupils to see that worth is determined by the appraiser, not by the intrinsic merit of the thing appraised. He decides its market value, what supply and demand are, whether it has monetary value. Ask if the pupils have any keepsakes they wouldn't part with for love or money. Why? Are there some things beyond a money value (like health)? What was the Holy Grail worth to the knights of King Arthur's court? Picture the value of the basin and towel left in the Upper Room after Jesus washed the disciples' feet.

2. Appraise the value of a man.

The pupil's book suggests a man's value in politics, in industry and business, in social life. The market value of the ingredients of a human body might be added—at most, a few dollars. (This whole theme may be tied in with a previous discussion of what bread is—its value and meaning determined by a variety of persons.)

3. Indicate God's appraisal.

The pupil's book will be your resource material here, too. You may ask pupils whether they feel bigger among others their own size or among giants. The higher the yardstick, the smaller we feel. And this is the surprise point here. Before God we have an impossible standard to meet, and one would expect the lowest rating to be given us. But the reverse is actually true. This is why, when God is ignored or deliberately left out, human values become cheaper, not more precious.

This will not be an easy point for pupils to grasp, but you can leave them with a curiosity about it, and the Bible passages will whet their curiosity even more.

4. Explore the Bible passages.

Questions to sharpen the study:

Matthew 10:28–31. What corresponds to the cheapness of sparrows today? How can an Almighty God take note of such trifles?

Luke 15:3–10. What gives the one sheep its value? How do things multiply their value by being lost?

John 3:16. How does this indicate man's value? Is it the same as that found in 1 John 3:1-3?

John 10:11–15. How can you tell sheep apart? Do you like to be an individual in your own right, or merely part of a group?

Matthew 20:20–28 and Luke 12:16–21. What gives man true worth? Do we measure success by service or by being served?

A summary of the passages may be attempted by pupils. Note that value depends on how much a person matters, is wanted, and is needed. Note the individuality of God's view—seeing us as persons, not as things. Underscore our value to him because he made and loves us.

5. Examine the Confession of Sins in The Service.

Give special attention to the Declaration of Grace: "power to become the sons of God." Have one pupil lead the class in using the confessional paragraphs as they would on Sunday morning.

Ask pupils to look for a bifocal view here: on the one hand, acknowledging our sinfulness without a claim on God's goodness; on the other hand, being declared a son of God. How a person can be both sinner and saint at one and the same moment remains a mystery.

88

Yet this is God's view of us—sinners because of our unworthiness, saints because of his grace.

6. Hear reports on human rights.

If no pupil has volunteered for this research project, it may be omitted under pressure of time. Or you might open it up as an application of the "worth of man."

Where are human rights being infringed today? Examples of oppression of minority groups, of playing favorites, or of denying privileges of law and protection may be cited. Are there rights we should uphold for humans wherever and whoever they are?

Milestones in human rights include abolition of slavery, changing the inferior status of women, removing the penalty for debts, hospitalizing the sick and handicapped, and providing social welfare legislation.

7. See the implication of viewing people as things.

Examples may be shown of what happens when God is left out, e.g., the use of humans as agents of the state or to form armies or slave working forces (the children of Israel in the land of Egypt) or the cheapness of human life to factory owners who provide no safety devices or medical care for the protection of employees. Contrast this with the view that each person is a child of God for whom Christ died.

8. Make assignments for the next session.

Assign Chapter 12. Check on research reports.

---

session 12
SCOPE OF SESSION

Beginning with this session the personal application of Luther's explanation of the First Article comes to the fore. This session sets forth the premise "I am his" and introduces a stewardship emphasis. Succeeding sessions (especially Session 14) will consider the "so what" of this initial premise.

Stewardship here is viewed as response to God's ownership of all of a person's life. It sets the work of God the Father in personal terms—what it means to a specific individual and to share God's free gifts.

MATERIALS NEEDED

Bibles. Pupil's book (Chapter 12).

AN OVERVIEW OF THE SESSION

1. *Discuss to whom a child belongs. You may have research reports here.*
2. *Have the class say Luther's explanation of the First Article of the Creed.*

3. Reweigh Luther's explanation, casting it against claims indicated in the previous discussion. Use the pupil's book (Chapter 12) as an explanation.
4. Examine Bible passages for the claims of God on us as his children.
5. Summarize with a statement showing the personal nature of the First Article—"I believe," not "we believe."
6. Make assignments for the next session.

SESSION PLAN IN GREATER DETAIL

1. Discuss "Who owns a child?"

The discussion here will not only launch the session, but can become almost the heart of the session. If you include the suggested questions and research reports and the material in Chapter 12 of the pupil's book, more than half the session time could be allotted here.

Instances of competing claims upon a child may be cited briefly: the state's taking the child out of the home to train in its own ideology; the demands of a school on a child's time beyond the defined school hours; the rights of parents to have children excused from school; the state's right to have a child vaccinated to safeguard public health; the church's right to educate a child in its doctrines and practices.

Some pupils may be asked to pose as judges of such cases, other pupils presenting evidence pro and con. Their decision will be their answer to the question "Whose is the child?" They will be deciding priorities among the state, the family, the school, the church, and society.

Ask pupils to give research reports on conflicts of interest. Use the chalkboard to list various claims on pupils. Let them list eight or ten, such as school, hobbies, church, family, sports, earning money. Ask in what order of priority they would list these items if they had a choice. Their list will show the priority given each claim. (Avoid the simple answer "The church always comes first.")

If research pupils have no reports to make, present a case or two of your own. Take the parents who refuse to send their children to public school, claiming they can educate them better themselves. How would you judge their case? Or, here's a parent who for reasons of conscience refuses to have his child given a blood transfusion; doctors claim their refusal may cost the child his life. How would you judge the case?

You may follow this by asking if we can ever do things "on our own time." How will they regard what their "own time" is? Does a man's activity after working hours have any bearing on his work? Can his employer tell him where he is to live, what clubs to join, what debts he may incur, what rules of health to observe? What claims does the employer have on non-working hours? These questions funnel into the broader question "Whose Am I?"

2. Lead a recital of Luther's explanation.

Try leading your pupils in repeating Luther's explanation of the First Article of the Creed without using their books. You can put a few key words on the chalkboard as reminders and erase them as they are no longer needed.

This is largely a memory exercise, requiring not more than a few minutes. Laggards will be carried along in unison repetition from memory. This exercise will serve as a change of pace after the previous discussion, and as a bridge to the closer study of Luther's explanation.

3. Reweigh Luther's explanation.

In this step refer to appropriate sections of Chapter 12 to focus the discussion on three points: (a) Luther's emphasis on creation as an ongoing act, not a past act alone; (b) God's use of natural means as an agent of his creative work; and (c) God's claim on us, as stated in the final two sections.

Faith healing might be used as an illustration of the second point (though with caution, lest it sidetrack the main issue and cease to be merely an illustration). We regard both faith and medicine as God's healing agents; a common attitude would separate them, as though faith implied a disparaging of medicine.

The third point could end with a reference to Matthew 10:34–37. Pupils would see Christ's claims here, and be ready to move into the study of other passages.

4. Explore Bible passages.

The seven passages here reinforce God's claims upon us both as his creatures and as his children. Two of them (Matthew and Acts) deal with specific calls to discipleship and service. The 1 Corinthians passage applies God's ownership to our bodies. All the passages bear upon the section "Created Me!" in Chapter 12 of the pupil's book. Time will dictate how many passages you can handle.

In dealing with these passages, ask pupils to seek out their special point of reference to "I am his." They may answer: "Because he has made us"; "Because he has called us"; "Because he is our God." Galatians 6 suggests a responsibility God places on us as his children.

5. Summarize.

In a sentence or two, remind pupils of the difference between the pronouns used in the Lord's Prayer and those used in the Creeds. Whereas the former uses the plural "our" and "us," uniting us in a group prayer, the Creed uses "I," as though this must be a statement of personal belief that no one can assume for us.

6. Make assignments for the next session.

Ask the pupils to read Chapter 13 and to think about what God does for us. Check on research reports. Are the appointed pupils prepared for the debate? If not, help them get ready.

session 13
SCOPE OF SESSION

The study of Luther's explanation of the First Article continues here with an emphasis on the three *p*'s: preserves, provides, protects. The idea of God's providence comes under scrutiny, and Bible passages are directed toward that idea. This session also will anticipate Session 15 dealing with the fatherhood of God.

MATERIALS NEEDED

Pupil's book (Chapter 13). Bibles.

AN OVERVIEW OF THE SESSION

1. Reread Luther's explanation and underscore the three p's.
2. Have a debate.
3. Discuss the providence of God.
4. Explore Bible passages, partly to sharpen the issues, partly to get answers.
5. Conclude with a summary statement that God preserves like a father, provides like a father, protects like a father.
6. Make assignments for the next session.

SESSION PLAN IN GREATER DETAIL

1. Ascribe to God provision for needs.

Have the pupils reread Luther's explanation of the First Article of the Creed. Ask them for evidence of the three *p*'s ("preserves," "provides," "protects"). Ask if Luther's explanation makes sense in a world of science and natural law. How can we ascribe to God the provision for our needs when we know the natural factors that are at work?

Refer to factors like weather, soil, the labor market, problems of distribution of goods. The have and have-not nations might be cited: which nations lack for self-dependence, which nations have in abundance? How can things be evened up?

Material from the opening two sections of Chapter 13 of the pupil's book should be incorporated in the discussion.

2. Have a debate.

Seventh-graders are often unskilled in debate. (If this project was not assigned in advance, omit it.) Set a specific time limit for the presentation of both sides of the argument. Allow other pupils to cite their opinions when the debate is concluded.

The proposition: "Every man is entitled to all he can get, so long as he does it legally."

Statements pro and con should be made without entering into argument. Pupils should merely present the issue from both sides without trying to reach a verdict. Various economic systems will doubtless be mentioned: private enterprise and the profit incentive; socialism and the responsibility for have-nots; perhaps even communism.

A Christian's responsibility for others' needs underlies this debate and anticipates the study of Luke 16.

3. Discuss providence and the will of God.

Discuss the providence of God from another angle: Is everything that happens God's will? How do we decide what is and what isn't his will? (A deeper study of this question will come when pupils study "Thy will be done" in the next term.)

Luther's explanations of the Third and Fourth Petitions of the Lord's Prayer may be cited and read here. Note that God's will is always "good and gracious" and is done "without our prayer." Material from the final two sections of Chapter 13 of the pupil's book should be incorporated in this discussion.

Questions and problems need only be raised here, since the Bible passages should shed considerable light.

4. Explore Bible passages.

Use the following questions to stimulate discussion.

Psalm 91:1–12. Do promises here really hold water? Isn't it hollow to read such verses to sick people or those in real trouble? Is immunity the reward for loyalty?

Luke 16:19–31. What was the sin of the rich man? Is it wrong to have the wherewithal but do nothing to help? What link is there between this parable and the debate?

Luke 12:22–31. In what ways would God's care of birds and flowers describe his providence? Does this mean we can leave the work to God alone?

Psalm 23. How would this psalm describe God's role of preserver, provider, and protector? Note that he doesn't keep out of the valley or prevent enemies from approaching. What more does he do than spare us danger?

Exodus 16:13–21. An instance of God's provision. Would it make any difference if we knew that "manna" came through natural processes?

1 Corinthians 10:13. Could you restate this verse in simpler terms? (God provides strength equal to our needs.)

5. Formulate a summary statement.

While the relationship of father and child is implicit throughout this session, it has not been expressly stated. Thus, your summary statement should not go too deeply into this Father-child relationship, but merely anticipate its fuller treatment in Session 15.

Can pupils cite instances showing how human fathers preserve, provide, and protect? What if there were no father in the home? If the father were unemployed or handicapped?

6. Make assignments for the next session.

Assign reading of Chapter 14 and the Bible passages. Make sure research reports on full-time careers in the church will be ready.

---

session 14
SCOPE OF SESSION

This session deals with the outcome or application of the two previous sessions. Because "I am his" and because he preserves, provides, and protects, we are to "thank and praise, serve and obey him." This is viewed as his purpose for us, "what I am here for." Two biblical biographies, Joseph and Moses, are presented in the pupil's book as instances of God's purposes at work.

The stewardship emphasis is obvious, but largely in a sense of Christian vocation, of being called as Christians wherever we are and whatever we do.

MATERIALS NEEDED

Chalkboard. Bibles. Pupil's book (Chapter 14). Printed materials on church vocations and on the vocation of a Christian.

AN OVERVIEW OF THE SESSION

1. See God's guidance in the lives of Moses and Joseph.

2. Discuss God's guidance in other lives.

3. Explore Bible passages to see God's plan at work and to find examples of response to God's purposes.

4. Ask for a report from research pupils on full-time careers in the church. Discuss the report with pupils. Discuss factors that play a role in choosing a career.

5. Make a summary statement.

6. Make assignments for the next session.

SESSION PLAN IN GREATER DETAIL

1. See God's guidance in the lives of Moses and Joseph.

You may draw two series of objects on the chalkboard and ask pupils to decipher them. One series will have a coat, prison bars, a sheaf of wheat, and a crown. The other will have some cattails, a knife, a shepherd's crook, a fire, and a lamb. One suggests signal events in Joseph's life, the other in Moses' life. Ask pupils to fill in the Bible stories of these two men, using the chalkboard objects as cues.

If pupils have read Chapter 14, they should see the connection quickly. Offer no clues, however, unless they get stuck. (Knife refers to Moses' killing the Egyptian; lamb refers to the Passover and God's rescue of his people.)

The pupil's book suggests how "accidental" rearing of Moses in the Egyptian palace helped him later on, and how "accidental" shepherding equipped him to lead the Israelites. Try not to get sidetracked with the question of whether these events were predetermined or decreed by God. Point out how God uses the situations in which people find themselves as a part of his plan. The same procedure can be followed with the story of Joseph (how coincidental that he be imprisoned when the butler and baker were there!). We believe not that God manipulates people like puppets on strings, but that he guides them to make the best use of their opportunities.

2. Discuss God's guidance in other lives.

Can the pupils suggest other biblical examples, e.g. Paul? Paul's qualifications for missionary work: his tremendous drive, his intelligence, and his alertness to the world of Romans and Jews. The very factors that made him an ardent enemy of Christianity were used by God to advance the gospel.

How about non-biblical examples? Your own path to teaching? The factors that led the pastor into the ministry? Admit that events, taken together, may be a collection of accidents without meaning or purpose; yet they take on special meaning when related to God's purpose. People are not puppets, with events of their lives chronicled in advance in some secret book. It's rather when their lives are related to God that plan and purpose begin to be seen.

In setting forth these examples, keep the father image in mind. How far does a father go in charting his child's life? Up to a point he may decide for the child. But comes the day when his "charting" consists of talking things over, offering advice, giving support, and approving—but the decisions rest with the child.

3. Explore Bible passages.

Since your review of Joseph and Moses has involved biblical material, you may defer this section until you have completed the study of Christian vocation.

The first passage (Nehemiah 9:9–15) shows a Bible interpretation of events of history, whereas the other six passages deal primarily with stewardship. If pupils like puzzle gimmicks, you might ask them to complete the following statement, using the final six Bible passages as cues: "Because I am his, and because he preserves me, provides for me, and protects me, . . ."

4. Discuss and hear reports on Christian vocation.

While the emphasis of Christian vocation is on being called as a Christian in any kind of work, there are implications for considering career possibilities. (The full consideration of careers will come at a later date, so don't feel that you must explore the subject deeply here.) Refer to the section "The Call" in the pupil's book.

Factors usually considered in choosing a career may be listed on the chalkboard: prestige, money, good working conditions, own boss, helping others, advancement. Let pupils add others. In what order of importance will pupils list them?

Some attention may be given to service opportunities in various non-church careers, underscoring the motive of service as a choice factor. Pupils may be asked what their present leanings are, and why they are so inclined.

If research pupils give no report on church vocations, attention should be given through pupil discussion. What "image" do they have of the ministry, parish work, music director, Christian education director? Do they know what the academic requirements are? The service opportunities? The kinds of work done by each? The satisfactions and drawbacks of each?

5. Summarize the session.

Sum up the session. Emphasize "thanking and praising, serving and obeying" in all of life—the call to be Christian wherever we are.

6. Make assignments for the next session.

Ask pupils to read Chapter 15.

---

session 15
SCOPE OF SESSION

This session should gather together the main points of the entire unit's study of God as Father. Chapter 15 of the pupil's book serves as your guide, showing how the Creator is Father, how his provision and protection are roles of the Father, how the worth of man stems from God's love as Father, how God's power is an agent of his Fatherhood. Throughout the entire unit the Fatherhood of God has been emphasized, for it is only in this light that a Christian views God.

Since this session concludes the first term, you may want to devote time to completing unfinished items. Conclude with the use of the check test as an evaluation tool.

MATERIALS NEEDED

Bibles. Pupil's book (Chapter 15). Papers with pupils' original answers to the check test.

AN OVERVIEW OF THE SESSION

1. *Talk about what the word "father" means.*
2. *Ask researchers for reports on Jesus' teaching about God.*
3. *Explore Bible passages. Emphasize Luke 15, one of the Bible's finest pictures of God. Underscore the idea of relationship—there can be no father without a child.*
4. *Discuss the material from Chapter 15 of the pupil's book*

dealing with current problems in thinking of God as personal and caring.

5. Have pupils complete check test again to see whether they agree with their reactions made at the opening of the unit or have made some changes in their thinking.

6. Conclude the unit with a summary.

7. Make assignments for the next session.

SESSION PLAN IN GREATER DETAIL

1. Have pupils give their idea of a "father."

Ask what the word "father" suggests to pupils. What has it meant at other times and in other lands? Do pupils feel an aloofness in "father" that isn't present in "daddy"? Review Luther's explanation of the First Article, emphasizing "paternal." Through a quick review of preceding sessions, ask how God's fatherhood has shown through in every session.

Against current picture of fathers—one hardly ever at home, another playing on all fours with a child—describe an old photo showing father seated and mother standing, her hand resting on his shoulder. In those days father's word was law, striking fear and obedience into the child's heart.

You might ask why Jesus didn't use "mother" for God, if love is his chief quality. Is there a sense of justice and sternness in "father"?

2. Examine Jesus' teaching about God.

If the research pupils have worked on this with a concordance, they may give their reports. Otherwise you may deal with this briefly, using the following as a guide.

The Gospel of John has frequent allusions to God as Father, mostly in relationship with Jesus as Son. Bible passages in John 14 and 5 may be explored to sum up this relationship.

Ask why Jesus said so little about God as Creator and Almighty. Jesus undoubtedly assumed belief in God in these roles. His listeners needed nothing further on this score, except to know God pre-eminently as Father. The latter doesn't replace the former; it merely puts the creative work of an almighty God in its proper perspective.

3. Explore Bible passages.

Luke 15:11–32 is the key here. Ask pupils to note: the worth of the wayward son in the eyes of the father; the freedom of choice given the wayward son; the persistent seeking by the father; the pride and selfishness of the two sons; the difference in attitude between the elder brother and the father toward the prodigal. Jesus gave no title to this story. Is it right to call it the Parable of the Prodigal if the father is the real hero? How would pupils rename the story?

Hosea 11:1–4 indicates an Old Testament view of God as Father and anticipates the New Testament teaching. Ephesians 3:14–19 is Paul's prayer to the Father for the blessing of believers.

4. Discuss how God can be a personal God.

Chapter 15 is important; talk about it. How can people know God personally? Here you may refer to a common view; some people think that God is nothing more than spirit and energy, somewhat like electricity, a force behind the universe. By what boldness can we claim God's personal interest in us? Here you may set God against the staggering vastness of outer space, with the world as a mere speck, and ask if such a God can possibly care for man. Only because Christ revealed him as Father can we dare call ourselves children!

5. Have pupils do the check test again.

This is to see if pupils' views have changed during these sessions. It provides a good evaluation for your teaching, too! As at the end of the preceding unit, ask pupils to place their answers in a second column on their papers and add comments to explain their answers if they wish. If there is time, discuss their answers, with special emphasis on ideas which have changed during the unit.

6. Summarize the first term.

While the check test may provide an adequate tool for summary, you may want to make up a brief quiz to cover the entire term (especially Units B and C) and also ask for an evaluation of strong and weak spots of the course.

7. Make assignments for the next session.

Allow a few moments at the very end to anticipate coming studies. Beginning next session, pupils will turn from matters of faith and the First Article of the Creed to matters of worship and the Lord's Prayer. Ask them to read Chapter 16 for the next session.

SECTION 4

SECTION FOUR

Teaching Plans for Term 2

UNIT D:
prayer

UNIT OBJECTIVES

1. To help the pupil understand the nature of prayer.

2. To help him become more familiar with forms used in prayer, including classic forms in hymnal and liturgy.

3. To help him grow in the habit of praying.

SCOPE OF UNIT

This unit has a threefold function: (1) to serve as a bridge between the two terms; (2) to introduce term-long projects such as the Prayer Notebook; and (3) to launch the pupil's study of private and public worship.

Little time need be allowed for the "bridge" function—no more than is needed to give a perspective view of the year's pattern: "I believe . . . I respond." The sessions on prayer will underscore this repeatedly and show how the response of worship is the natural sequel to faith in God as Father.

Considerably more time will be needed to outline term-long studies and projects. These are sketched out in the sections "Prayer Notebook," "Memorizing the Catechism," and "Worship." Their inclusion in this unit introduction does not mean that they apply only to the two sessions on prayer. They should be extended throughout the term as ongoing areas of research and study.

Obviously, two sessions will be inadequate for dealing with the many aspects of prayer. Many aspects can await the next unit, which treats of the Lord's Prayer. In this particular unit, limit yourself to:

1. The nature of prayer, which grows out of relationship with God as Father.

2. Types of prayer, including free and formal prayers, confession, petition, intercession, and thanksgiving.

3. Habits of prayer, including time, place, procedures, postures, and patterns.

4. Difficulties in prayer, including how to handle distractions; questions such as "Does God answer prayer?"

STRUCTURE OF THE UNIT

Normally a unit should be compressed within fixed time limits. However, this unit bears such a close relationship to the unit on the Lord's Prayer that a special degree of flexibility is suggested. Instead of concluding "Prayer" in two sessions, combine your study of "Prayer" and the "Lord's Prayer" through a nine-session span.

If provocative questions stimulate your pupils to think and express their own personal feelings, perhaps you can structure parts of the sessions around discussion questions. Here are a few, to which you might add others culled from the pupil's book:

Is the saying of prayers the same as praying?

Has the value of prayer shrunk as our knowledge of natural law has expanded?

If Jesus attacked "vain repetitions," should we avoid read or memorized prayers?

Is the aim of prayer to get what we couldn't get otherwise?

What should a person expect from prayer?

Is habit the enemy of true prayer?

In what ways does our view of God color our praying?

These discussions will be more productive if the pupils are familiar with the material in their reading books. You might, therefore, ask pupils to study and think through both chapters of this unit prior to the class sessions.

Laboratory time should be planned in each session for Bible study, help with sentence prayers and worship, and the Prayer Notebook (see below).

MATERIALS NEEDED

Bibles and service books will be needed in all sessions throughout the term. The service book (a copy for each pupil) should be that used in the public worship of your church (when the *Service Book and Hymnal* is specifically referred to here, find the corresponding item in your own service book, if it differs).

You might make books of prayers available for resource and browsing purposes. You could include collections of formal prayers for public worship and collections for private devotions.

If uniform Prayer Notebooks are desired, they should be on hand for the opening session. Suggestions are offered below for type, style, and size.

PRAYER NOTEBOOK

A Prayer Notebook is a laboratory tool for this entire term. Uniform notebooks will make the project something special—to be treasured and used long after the term ends. A nice binder 5½ by 8½ inches, with top or side hinge and fastener, is available for about $4.00 per dozen in stationery stores. Sheets could be cut, punched, and fastened in advance, providing a permanent stiff-back notebook. Pupils who prize nice things could put their notebooks in typed form later on. Pictures or original art work could be added to capture visually the mood of a prayer.

Pupils could include in the Prayer Notebook:

1. Great collects of the church, including those listed below (under "classic Prayers").

2. Other brief prayers used in public worship, such as Luther's Morning and Evening Prayers.

3. Prayers for special occasions, such as table graces.

4. Stanzas of hymns that lend themselves to personal prayer use.

5. Sentence prayers prepared by pupils.

6. Prayers found and liked by pupils.

7. Psalms and Bible passages that lend themselves to prayer use, perhaps in such categories as trust, thanksgiving, confession, intercession.

Prayer Hymns

Since a search for prayers among hymns may seem like looking for a needle in a haystack, a partial selection of hymns in prayer form is offered here. Hymn numbers refer to the *Service Book and Hymnal.*

Prayers for the church: (153) "Jesus, with thy Church abide," (157) "Lord of our life, and God of our salvation."

Before worship: (188) "Lord Jesus Christ, be present now."

Close of worship: (191) "Lord, dismiss us with thy blessing."

Morning: (209) "God of our life, all-glorious Lord."

Evening: (221) "Saviour, breathe an evening blessing," (223) "All praise to thee, my God this night," (227) "The day thou gavest, Lord, is ended."

Work: (213) "Behold us, Lord, a little space."

Personal dedication: (289) "O God, accept my heart this day," (538) "Lord, speak to me, that I may speak," (507) "Jesus, Master, whose I am," (511) "Thine for ever! God of love," (515) "O Jesus, I have promised," (510) "Take my life, and let it be."

Personal guidance: (520) "Guide me, O thou great Jehovah," (532) "Jesus, still lead on."

Help in temptation: (561) "In the hour of trial."

Thanksgiving and adoration: (444) "For the beauty of the earth," (448) "O Lord of heaven and earth and sea," (403) "Lord, with glowing heart I'd praise thee," (434) "Beautiful Saviour, King of Creation."

Confession: (365) "Lord Jesus, think on me," (386) "O Jesus, thou art standing."

102

For the needy: (351) "Where cross the crowded ways of life."
For the nation: (345) "Not alone for mighty empire," (340) "From ocean unto ocean."
For absent loved ones: (337) "Holy Father, in thy mercy."
For personal needs: (472) "Lead us, O Father, in the paths of peace," (489) "O God, I love thee," (504) "Jesus, my Lord, my God, my all," (451) "Teach me, my God and King," (467) "Dear Lord and Father of mankind."

Classic Prayers

Certain fine collects also may be included in the Prayer Notebooks. Of the collects listed below, the starred ones are universal favorites; others are given for personal taste. Numbers refer to pages in the *Service Book and Hymnal.*

*233   *For Purity:* "Almighty God, unto whom all hearts are open"

*140   *For Grace:* "O Lord, our heavenly Father"

*148   *For Peace:* "O God, from whom all holy desires"

*233   *For Divine Assistance:* "Direct us, O Lord, in all our doings"

*233   *For the Spirit of Prayer:* "O Almighty God, from whom every good prayer cometh"

231   *For Love to God:* "O God, who has prepared for them that love thee"

218   *For the Church:* "Most gracious Father, we humbly beseech thee"

230   *For Divine Protection:* "O Lord, support us all the day long"

231   *For Guidance:* "O Lord God, who hast called us"

235   *In Time of Affliction:* "Lord, who knowest the deep places"

91   *In Affliction:* "O God, who makest the minds of the faithful to be of one will"

154   *Luther's Morning Prayer:* "We give Thanks to Thee, heavenly Father"

155   *Luther's Evening Prayer:* "We give Thanks to Thee, heavenly Father"

Also the following collect: "Teach us, good Lord, to serve thee as thou deservest; to give and not to count the cost; to fight and not to heed the wounds; to toil and not to seek for rest; to labor and not to ask for any reward, save that of knowing that we do thy will; through Jesus Christ our Lord."

Sentence Prayers

You may find considerable timidity among pupils about expressing themselves publicly in prayer. Even though they do pray, and don't mind joining in group prayer, they may feel self-conscious about voicing personal prayers. This is a place to exercise considerable understanding and guidance. Several suggestions are offered here to surmount pupils' awkwardness:

1. Help each pupil to feel that awareness of God's presence comes before all else. He is praying to God, not to others in the group. Guide him in praying as though God and he, the pray-er, were the only ones present.

2. Help your pupils to move through gradual stages. They may begin by reading aloud some of the prayers they have written down in their Prayer Notebooks. Then ask them to write out a sentence prayer of their own. Have them put this prayer aside when the time

comes for them to pray it in the group and not try to remember all the words they had written, but concentrate on expressing the key thoughts. Then ask them to offer a sentence prayer without writing anything down in advance.

3. Set the example yourself. You might initiate a period of free prayer in worship with a prayer of your own. Later ask various pupils to join in with prayers of their own.

4. Provide them with certain key thoughts in praying—thoughts of thanksgiving, petition and need, intercession or prayer for others. Encourage them to be specific in prayers for such areas. What do they have to be thankful for? What needs do they have? What conditions or needs of others can they think of?

Exercises in sentence prayers should begin early in the term. Pupils might be asked to prepare and hand in a brief prayer of thanksgiving, petition, or intercession. You may then have a personal conference with pupils to help them to express themselves better.

You might also ask for written prayers keyed to certain life experiences—preparing to eat a meal, celebrating a birthday, facing a rough problem, having a disagreement with a friend, entering church, feeling discouraged.

PRIVATE DEVOTIONS

Your encouraging and guiding pupils in private devotions will be a term-long concern. While private devotions involve extra-session time, some attention could be given in the class sessions to helping the pupils develop their personal devotional life. Review their progress from time to time.

Ask pupils to set aside a certain time each day for private devotions. If the group as a whole could agree on a time, it would give each pupil a sense of oneness with the group in private prayer.

Pupils might discuss what should be included in such a period of private devotions. The text of Luther's *Small Catechism* offers one pattern. Another may be found in devotional booklets available in most churches. Whatever the pattern, ask that they hold to it consistently over the weeks of the term at least.

Scripture reading and prayer should be the core of the devotions. This means listening to God's Word and responding in prayer. Bible readings could be part of this daily devotional period. It might be supplemented with a psalm a day, with psalms in prayer form, or with psalms included in the service book. Sentence or free prayers should be used, together with classic forms of prayers from their Prayer Notebooks. The devotional period could follow a simple outline: daily Bible reading; psalm; silence and free prayer; collect or classic form of prayer; Lord's Prayer.

MEMORIZING THE CATECHISM

It's difficult to escape using rote memorization in this term. You may incorporate Luther's explanations of the Lord's Prayer into group worship (prefixing to each explanation "I believe that . . . ," thus making each an affirmation of faith). But if one explanation were used in each session, you would still cover all nine explanations only twice— not often enough to know by heart.

Several possibilities may be suggested:

1. Reduce the volume of material to be learned by rote. Use only four explanations in group worship (The Introduction and the first three petitions). By the fourth round, these should be fairly well known.

2. Memorize the explanations yourself, and then pass on to pupils the key words and phrases (such as Luther's frequent "the devil, the world, and our sinful self") that aided your memorization.

3. Stagger the memorization over the entire term by memorizing one explanation every two weeks. If pupils can maintain a schedule of one explanation per week, they will be simultaneously memorizing and studying the Lord's Prayer, and thus mesh their memorizing with session studies.

4. Use abler pupils to help the slower. You might want to have memorization periods during class sessions.

WORSHIP

Group worship should be both a laboratory for constructing services and a period of group devotion. All pupils should take part, perhaps working in pairs, with assignments and dates set at the beginning of the term. Each pair is free to select or construct its own pattern. You may want to offer guidance on:

1. The use of orders included in the service book. Matins and Vespers depend on the time of day. Suffrages could be used, as well as the Bidding Prayer and the Litany. Care should be taken to follow instructions given in the service book for these orders.

2. Scripture passages to be used. Daily Bible readings may provide an occasional source, likewise passages appointed for Matins or Vespers in the service book.

3. The bare core of group devotions: Scripture reading, prayer, and The Lord's Prayer.

4. Themes for worship. This requires resourcefulness, and challenges abler pupils. Hymns, Bible passage, prayer, and a poem or thought for the day should all follow a single theme. If pupils respond to this type of worship, suggest themes that will tie in with various sessions: Prayer, Reverence, Kingdom of God, Daily Bread, Forgiveness, Temptation, Praise.

106

5. Some uniform practices in worship. Psalms should always be followed by speaking or singing the Gloria Patri. The group should stand for prayer. Hymns should be spaced out over the period of worship.

6. The necessity of advance preparation. You might suggest that pupils submit plans a week in advance, just to make sure everything is in order.

7. Possible use of memorization material.

---

session 16
SCOPE OF THE SESSION

Part of this session will preview the whole term's study of worship and outline areas for research and group participation. It will also guide pupils in their private devotions and in preparing for leadership in group worship.

In dealing with prayer in this session, assume that your pupils are already praying, at least at bedtime, meals, and public worship. Many pupils, even now, will be using prayers learned in early childhood. Your purpose, therefore, will be to help pupils grow more skillful in expressing themselves in prayer, in linking their prayer life more closely with their faith, and in filling their prayer life with vitality.

Regard this session and the next as a single unit, taking up next week where you finish this week.

MATERIALS NEEDED

Bibles. Service Books. Hymnals. Prayer Notebooks. Pencils. Pupil's book (Chapter 16).

AN OVERVIEW OF THE SESSION

1. *Introduce and explain some of the term-long activities.*
2. *Discuss the way and how and why of prayer, using the pupil's book, together with the suggestions outlined below as resources.*
3. *Explore the examples of Christ in prayer cited in the Bible passages.*
4. *Explain the Prayer Notebook. If time permits, ask pupils to begin work on their notebooks, using the* Service Book and Hymnal *as a resource.*
5. *Make assignments for the next session.*

SESSION PLAN IN GREATER DETAIL

1. Introduce activities.

Use the unit introduction as your guide. Talk about such activities as group worship, memorization, sentence prayers, and private devotions. Do not go into them in detail; defer discussing other items of the unit introduction until they relate to specific sessions.

At this point in the session you may also want to deal with the Prayer Notebook. If so, revise the sequence of steps accordingly.

2. Discuss prayer.

The core of the session lies in this discussion. For your own preparation reread the theological background article "Prayer and the Lord's Prayer" (especially the first half) and Chapter 16 of the pupil's book.

To launch the discussion, you might want to use the pupil's book as a guide, asking for reactions to each section and proposing relevant questions. Or you may begin by asking what good it does to pray. Do we continue to pray only out of habit, because it's a ritual learned in early childhood? Pupils may respond that prayer brings peace of mind or that it offers a certain release from problems and tensions. If they suggest that prayer doesn't depend on the good it may do, pick up this point and pursue it. Show them a parallel of prayer as a response. Have your pupils imagine themselves outside a football stadium, listening to the sounds of the crowd. Where cheers reflect an appreciation of the play on the field, prayers reflect an appreciation of God's encounter with us. Or you might liken prayer to communication in a home, asking your pupils what good it does to talk to a parent. The value of the communication is not governed by what "good" it may do.

Another approach might be asking how many pupils swim. How did they learn—by being pushed into the water or by taking a swimming class? Would it be better to develop one's own style first and then have experts revise it? Or start with the experts? The application to prayer should be obvious. First we pray in a fumbling, routine way, but then prayer begins to have vitality. In both instances, we learn by doing.

Or you might ask what prayer is—what is its purpose? Is it a way to get something we couldn't get otherwise? A superstitious carryover from olden days? A tossing of thoughts and words into the air? What is the key to prayer? Is it in getting what we ask? In feeling better? Or in the kind of God we worship?

During the discussion you may want to cite some cases, asking pupils what is right and wrong in each case. Here are a few samples:

a) A salesman who is habitually late for appointments leaves his packing until the last minute and then prays that the train will be late. The time he spends on his knees might well be used in getting to the station on time. Is this a misuse of prayer?

b) Miners are trapped in a cave-in. After frantic efforts, a few of the trapped miners are rescued. They regard their rescue as an answer to their prayers. How about the others who also prayed but weren't rescued?

c) A skier thanks God for a sudden snowstorm that makes the skis runs fast. How about the fellow whose car is stuck in a snow drift?
d) The mother of James and John asked the Lord to favor her boys with a special place in the kingdom (Matthew 20:20-24). The other disciples resented this request. Was her prayer misguided?

Don't ask pupils to pass judgment on the pray-ers. Merely ask if such prayers were proper. Were they inclined to be selfish? Should they have prayed differently? Would the same results have come without praying? Should deep personal need be the major concern of praying?

Don't press for fixed conclusions to such questions. They should stimulate thought, opening the way to the point of view set forth in the pupil's book—that prayer is our normal response to the love God has for us, whether it does us good or gets what we ask or performs miracles.

Raise the question of the place of prayer in the world of science. The pupil's book deals with this briefly. The answer, of course, lies in how we view prayer. If prayer's purpose is to get something by divine intervention, then its point has been blunted by our expanding our scientific knowledge. Of course we must remember that God, the Creator of all natural laws, can use those natural laws to answer prayer. If prayer is communication with the God of love, then our knowledge of the world won't affect it.

To feel the sharpness of prayer as communication, ask pupils if they have ever clammed up and refused to speak to a member of their family. How did they feel about it? What caused it? Were they happy or unhappy over it? Indicate that the same reaction ensues when communication with God is cut off—the withering of the spiritual life, isolation from God, loss of the reality of God.

3. Explore Bible passages.

The Bible passages referred to in the pupil's book report situations in which our Lord prayed: before choosing his closest friends; at the decisive moment of transfiguration; on raising Lazarus from the dead; in the trial at Gethsemane; after the return of the seventy followers he sent out to preach the gospel; when Peter confessed him as Christ; in the midst of a miracle. Each was a special time. You might ask what situations would be comparable for the pupils. Choosing and dealing with friends? Moments of great decision? Temptations and tough problems? Success? Mealtime? What kind of prayer would a person offer for such special situations?

Since the seven passages illustrate a point, they are not meant for close study. Don't spend much time on any single passage.

4. Explain the Prayer Notebook.

In this session you can probably go no further than acquainting pupils with the treasury of prayers in the Bible and hymnal. Limit their present search to hymns and psalms. Ask if they can identify a psalm in prayer form, or a hymn in prayer form. Usually the use of the second person ("thee" or "thou" or "thy") is the clue. They can locate many such examples by leafing through Psalms. You might list the numbers of several prayer hymns given in the unit introduction on the chalkboard and have pupils study them.

Next, help them see how psalms not presently in prayer form can be adapted. Psalm 23 would be an example, Psalm 103 another. (O Lord, thou art my shepherd, etc.; thou forgivest all our iniquity, thou healest all our diseases, etc.)

Pupils will need some guidance in selecting hymns and psalms for special prayer use. Headings in the hymnal could be read hastily for this. Opening lines of hymns and psalms also provide a clue. Psalms 51 and 150 might be used as examples of opening lines—in one instance, beginning a prayer of confession, in the other a prayer of adoration and thanksgiving.

If time permits, pupils may write a few mealtime prayers in their Prayer Notebook. They may want to include Psalm 103:1–2 and adapt Psalm 145:15–16 for table grace use.

5. Make assignments for the next session.

Ask the pupils to read Chapter 17 and particularly to study the Bible passages to find examples of petition, confession, and intercession.

---

session 17
SCOPE OF SESSION

Whereas the previous session established the need and the basis for prayer, this session will deal with types of prayers, regularity of praying, formal and free prayers, spoken and silent prayers. Chapter 17 of the pupil's book could be used as a guide to these emphases.

If the discussion questions posed in "Structure of the Unit" in the unit introduction have been followed, this session will continue questions begun last week. Introduce the matters of types of prayers, regularity of praying, and formal and free prayers.

MATERIALS NEEDED

Bibles. Service books. Hymnals. Prayer Notebooks. Pencils. Pupil's book (Chapter 17).

AN OVERVIEW OF THE SESSION

1. Using the pupil's book as a guide, discuss habits of prayer, types of prayer, formal and informal praying, spoken and silent prayers.

2. Explore Jesus' teachings on prayer through Bible study.

3. Continue work on the Prayer Notebook. Emphasize collects, especially the form used in constructing a collect.

4. Help pupils to construct sentence prayers.

5. Make assignments for the next session.

SESSION PLAN IN GREATER DETAIL

1. Discuss various uses and forms of prayer.

The use and misuse of such rote prayers as Ave Maria, Pater Noster (the Roman Catholic title of the Lord's Prayer), "Now I lay me" could be cited here. Note the emphasis of groups such as the Mohammedans on special hours of prayer. Ask about the dangers of rote praying. Can we learn something by heart and still not say it *from* the heart? You might also ask pupils to read Matthew 6:7–9, Matthew's setting for the Lord's Prayer. How can Jesus attack the use of "empty phrases" in verse 7, and then set forth a rote prayer for use by his own disciples? Isn't he advocating the very thing he just repudiated?

The initial section of Chapter 17 in the pupil's book raises the same issues. Would pupils agree with positions advanced there—that habit isn't necessarily bad, that they can pray even when "saying" prayers? Have they found their minds wandering during rote prayers (such as the Lord's Prayer) in public worship?

The use of free or formal prayers in worship sounds the same note. Ask pupils what risk they find in free prayer, in formal prayer. What safeguards should be made in each instance? (In free prayer, *all* needs should be included, not merely the pressing personal needs of the pray-er; in formal prayer, the prayer should come from the heart, not merely the lips.)

The pupil's book section on spoken and unspoken prayers merits attention. You might ask pupils to refer to the opening lines of Psalm 139, indicating that God reads the mind and heart. Pose the question: If God knows our needs and desires before we do, why pray? Compare such a situation with that of a human family where the father knows his child's needs before the child asks—but still wants to be asked.

Four kinds of prayers are mentioned in the pupil's book. These four types should be sufficient for pupils. Can pupils identify prayers of confession, intercession, thanksgiving, petition? The Prayer of the Church (*Service Book and Hymnal,* page 6) might be examined for these types. Note that confession is more implied than direct in this prayer. (You might point to the prayers of confession in the confessional services as examples.) Perhaps a few hymns could be examined to classify the type of prayer voiced in the hymn.

In dealing with these types, pupils should see how they mesh in forming a well-balanced prayer. While the major note may be thanksgiving, the prayer could also include confession, intercession, and petition.

2. Explore Bible passages.

The search for examples of various types of prayer may be carried over to exploration of Bible passages. Ask what each passage exemplifies. There are several instances of petition, one of confession, one of intercession.

Pupils might also be asked which passages point to sincerity of prayer, persistence in prayer, the power of prayer, the necessity of prayer.

3. Work on the Prayer Notebooks.

Outline for pupils the structure of a collect. Collects begin with a form of address, add a descriptive word or phrase, offer a brief petition, indicate the result of their petition, and conclude in the name of Christ. Use the collect *For Peace* as an example to help pupils see how a collect hangs together. Pupils might examine a group of collects in the service book to see what similarities they can find among them.

If you wish, copy the page numbers and titles of collects listed in the unit introduction and let pupils copy a few great collects in their Prayer Notebooks.

4. Help pupils construct sentence prayers.

Use the suggestions in the unit introduction for this. If you haven't initiated sentence prayers in worship, now is the time to spade the ground. You might suggest a theme—like thankfulness—and ask pupils to prepare a brief prayer on that theme. Other themes or situations might be added, with pupils working on prayers while you check their efforts.

5. Make assignments for the next session.

Ask pupils to read Chapter 18.

UNIT E:
the Lord's Prayer

UNIT OBJECTIVES

1. To help the pupil comprehend and accept the meaning and implications of each of the petitions of the Lord's Prayer for this life.

2. To help him understand the structure of the prayer in "Thy" and "us" petitions as well as its importance in public and private worship.

3. To encourage him to use the basic thoughts and key elements of the Lord's Prayer as a guide for his own praying.

SCOPE OF UNIT

The seven sessions of this unit focus on the Lord's Prayer. One session is designed for an over-all view of its structure, text, use, and place in Christian devotion; the remaining sessions offer a part-by-part study.

Your underlying purpose will be to help the pupil open his mind to the vast implications of each part of this model prayer. Do not try to dissect each petition (that could kill it!) or attempt to cover all the elements of the Christian faith and life; rather, try to breathe new life into well-worn words. If in the course of teaching these sessions you yourself don't find new, exciting insights, you can scarcely convey the spirit of this prayer to your pupils.

As indicated before, Unit D fuses into this unit. No transition is needed. The study of the Lord's Prayer is bound to be a study of prayer itself, for it provides the guide to well-rounded praying.

STRUCTURE OF THE UNIT

Teachers have commonly found the Lord's Prayer the most difficult part of the *Small Catechism* to teach effectively. Most of the difficulty lies in the breadth and sweep of this prayer. It encompasses the whole of the Christian life and expresses the whole of the Christian faith. The more you probe its implications of the whole of the Christian faith, the greater is its sweep. Be sure to read the theological background article "Prayer and the Lord's Prayer" carefully. Read Luther's explanation of the Lord's Prayer in the *Large Catechism* (embodied in the *Book of Concord*).

Two suggestions are offered to give your teaching sharpness. Follow the session-by-session plan, making each session a self-contained entity in a series. You will thus deal with seven distinct topics, each topic within a single session. The unit carry-over would then apply chiefly to notebook work, worship, memorization, and various review techniques.

The chapters in the pupil's book provide a teaching skeleton. You will find that the teaching guides for each session are more closely related to the pupil's book than in previous units—offering guides for its use, suggesting dominant emphases, drawing out points for discussion or further investigation. While the guidance material for each session is presented systematically for convenience, by no means feel that you must follow the suggested order. Adapt and adjust these suggestions to the needs and interests of your class. *Don't get into the rut of doing the same sort of thing at the same time in every class period.* This could be deadly.

The other suggestion is to underscore Luther's explanations which point to the heart of each part of the Lord's Prayer. This will keep the focus where it should be. If discussions tend to take the class somewhat afield, they should be deferred until the central truths have been explored adequately.

MATERIALS NEEDED

For the sessions, use the same materials as those listed in the introduction to Unit D.

PRAYER NOTEBOOK

As the various parts of the Lord's Prayer are studied, hymns and classic prayers that illustrate or express the various petitions should be sought out and written in the Prayer Notebooks. They need not be complete hymns, just a stanza or two that seems unusually appropriate.

Here is a list of appropriate prayer hymns. Numbers in parentheses refer to the *Service Book and Hymnal.*

First petition: (155) "Lord, keep us steadfast in thy word," (515) "O Jesus, I have promised."

Second petition: (329) "Thy kingdom come, O God," (318) "Thy kingdom come! O Father, hear our prayer."

Third petition: (580) "My Jesus, as thou wilt," (452) "Lord, teach us how to pray aright" (seventh stanza), (465) "My God and Father, while I stray."

Fourth petition: (444) "For the beauty of the earth," (448) "O Lord of heaven and earth and sea."

Fifth petition: (367) "With broken heart and contrite sigh," (370) "Just as I am, without one plea."

Sixth petition: (561) "In the hour of trial," (532) "Jesus, still lead on."

Seventh petition: (157) "Lord of our life," (520) "Guide me, O thou great Jehovah."

REPHRASING THE LORD'S PRAYER

A major project of this unit will be the rephrasing of the Lord's Prayer. Pupils' attempts to put the petitions into their own words could constitute the sentence prayers for this unit. These could be used in group worship as well as written in pupils' Prayer Notebooks.

This will not be an easy project for many of them, although they did much the same thing with the Apostles' Creed in the previous term. The very simplicity of the Lord's Prayer can become a roadblock. How else can you say, "Thy will be done"?

A before-and-after pattern (asking pupils to rephrase the petition before studying it and then to rephrase it again in the light of the study) may occasionally be used. This will give them a sense of achievement and help you know how clearly they understand the heart of the petition. You may not want to use this technique in each session, lest it become mechanical.

Another suggestion would be use a vocal exercise, asking just how the various petitions should be said. This may require a dramatic knack. How would a pupil say, "Thy will be done," for example? In a resigned sort of way? As though sweating out a tough decision? As though fighting against insuperable odds? As though leaving the door open, in case you didn't get your own way? As though to modify or qualify an impossible request? What inflection or emphasis would indicate these various moods? Or, to use the Fifth Petition as an example, what difference would be felt if the final "us" were given major emphasis? In how many ways could the petition be said? What would each way reflect?

(If this vocal exercise intrigues you, try it yourself first. Imagine yourself in a variety of situations, but still voicing the same petition. How would the Fifth Petition be expressed by a man with a terrible feeling of guilt? By a statesman voicing the feelings of a nation? By a person saying the petition automatically with his mind miles away? By David when confronted by Nathan? Try the same thing with other petitions.)

Or you might want to have pupils illustrate various parts of the Lord's Prayer. This activity would appeal to more creative pupils. Have them look for pictures that would capture the meaning or some aspect of the meaning of a particular petition. Magazine ads might be used here; or, if the pupil is artistically inclined, he could draw a symbolic illustration of his own. The petitions have seven themes, all somewhat difficult to put into picture form—reverence, hope, submission, thanksgiving, forgiveness, strength and courage, praise.

If your group likes this suggestion of pictures, have them begin their search early. Ask how they would picture these various themes, what sort of picture would they look for in each case. Rule out pictures that have distinctly biblical subjects (such as church art calendars or children's leaflets). Otherwise, don't attempt to channel their ideas, but rather appeal to their imagination. Ask that pupils who attempt this project have their picture with them on the date appointed for study of that petition.

Since the picture device strikes the central theme of each petition, it can also guide in rephrasing the Lord's Prayer. After each study ask for a summary statement of the petition by the whole class. How would they express its real meaning? When such a statement has been formulated (without an attempt to make it grammatically perfect), ask pupils to compare it with Luther's explanation, which is also a rephrasing of the petition. They may find that Luther's explanation puts their thoughts into words without their realizing it.

RESEARCH TOPICS

More gifted pupils may respond to an appeal for special investigation. Some topics are listed here to arouse their curiosity. Research projects should be placed on a voluntary basis, and topics need not be assigned at all if pupils do not respond. Offer of guidance should be given, and resources (for example, Bible dictionary and concordance) put at their disposal. Possible topics (with dates for reports) are:

What Jesus Meant by the Kingdom of God (Session 20)
*Can We Know God's Will for Us? (Session 21)
Explaining the Book of Job (Session 21)
*What's Unchristian About Fatalism? (Session 21)
*Why Pray for What We Can't Have? (Session 22)
Jesus' Teaching About Forgiveness (Session 23)

Starred topics do not involve Bible resource books, and will therefore, need special guidance. You might suggest that pupils ask church members these questions, think about answers themselves, confer with the pastor, and then assemble their findings.

Where a concordance or Bible dictionary is used, show pupils how to look for synonymous words. Thus "Devil" should be supplemented by "Satan" and "Tempter"; "kingdom of God" by "kingdom of heaven" and "king"; "forgiveness" by "sin" and "trespasses."

When pupils present their reports, you play the role of a moderator, posing questions that emerge from the topic, asking class members for their points of view, attempting to formulate general conclusions. Bear in mind, of course, that this may be a pupil's initial venture in preparing a topic. He may not probe the topic as deeply or cover it as extensively as you would like.

MEMORIZATION

Continue whatever memorization practices you decided on at the beginning of Unit D.

Note that the three "Thy" petitions are further explicated in the *Small Catechism* under the heading "When Does This Happen?" If these further meanings are added to the memorizing requirement, some attention should be given their content. All three encompass the whole of the Christian life; all three involve the Word of God—proclaiming it, living in harmony with it, believing in it, holding fast to it. The term "Word of God" itself may, therefore, require review, lest pupils make it synonymous with the Bible. (The class dealt with this subject in Session 7.) At an early point in the unit, go over the larger meaning of the "Word," suggesting it as anything and everything that communicates God's will and ways to us, whether the record of his deeds in Scripture, or his incarnation in Jesus Christ, or the proclaiming of his will and ways in preaching and teaching, or the unspoken word in the sacraments.

---

session 18

SCOPE OF SESSION

This session provides an overview of the Lord's Prayer. In addition to examining the structure, various wordings, and significance of the Lord's Prayer, try to excite interest in the more detailed study to follow in coming sessions.

MATERIALS NEEDED

Bibles. Pupil's book (Chapter 18 and *Small Catechism*). *Service Book and Hymnal.* Prayer Notebooks.

AN OVERVIEW OF THE SESSION

1. Introduce the Lord's Prayer by asking how well pupils think they know it.

2. Discuss the various sections of Chapter 18 of the pupil's book. Relevant Bible passages may be woven into this discussion.

3. Continue work in Prayer Notebooks by having pupils look for prayer hymns that express the spirit of prayer.

4. If a period of memorization is needed, set requirements and allow time for pupils to start their memorizing. (This can be a quiet-time period within the session as well as a homework assignment.)

5. Outline research projects for the unit (see the unit introduction). Ask for volunteers, set dates for reports, and offer such guidance as will apply to the whole group. (Help on individual assignments should not be given during class time.)

6. Make assignments for the next session.

SESSION PLAN IN GREATER DETAIL

1. Introduce the Lord's Prayer.

Ask if pupils can recall when they first learned the Lord's Prayer. What associations did they have then with such terms as "hallowed" and "heaven" and "kingdom"? Did they repeat syllables without knowing what they meant? Ask what ideas pop into their heads when they use such terms as "temptation," "trespasses," "daily bread." This will draw their interest and give you an idea of what concepts need correcting as you go along.

If pupils feel that they understand the words, merely indicate how much more the Lord's Prayer means to you now than when you were in the seventh grade, how well-worn words take on new color and come alive under a variety of circumstances. (You might take time to show how a single petition can be said in many different ways and with many different emphases—as suggested in the unit introduction.)

2. Use Chapter 18 of the pupil's book.

You may want to begin this study of what kind of prayer the Lord's Prayer is by making a cursory examination of some typical Old Testament prayers. To see the difference between the Lord's Prayer and typical Hebrew liturgical prayers for public worship, look at 1 Kings 8:15–53 (Solomon's prayer in dedicating the Temple) and at Nehemiah 9:6–37. To reinforce the point of the comparison, you might set Lincoln's Gettysburg Address against the two-hour oration Edward Everett delivered on the same occasion.

Turn to the information given in the pupil's book. The following subheadings correspond to those of the pupil's book and should be studied with Chapter 18.

"The Name of the Prayer"

Ask if anything in the Lord's Prayer would be offensive to other religious groups in school. If we wanted a common prayer, wouldn't the Lord's Prayer—acceptable to Jew, Mohammedan, and all but atheists —serve that purpose? Jesus' name appears nowhere. If this prayer were suddenly unearthed without its source being known, couldn't it be adopted as a prayer for men of every religion?

This will set the further question: Is it then a prayer for Christians alone? Note that it was given to the disciples, not to the masses of the people, that it has always been part of the worship of "the faithful," and that it is connected with the Lord's Supper.

Passages for Bible study may be examined here to show various Old Testament counterparts to petitions in the Lord's Prayer. How deliberately our Lord borrowed from the Old Testament here cannot be determined; it may strain a point to look for Old Testament sources. However, the Old Testament references illustrate the fact that Jesus gave old teachings new life and meaning.

Ask pupils to relate Bible verses to appropriate petitions. Examine only two passages in closer detail (Exodus 20:7 and 1 Chronicles 29:10–13).

"Various Wordings"

If pupils visit other churches or youth groups, they will soon learn the minor differences in words used for the Lord's Prayer. Some Christians say "debts," others say "trespasses"; some say "forever," others add "and ever." These word variations actually involve no difference in meaning. The extra "and ever," for example, doesn't make "forever" last any longer, but merely gives a kind of rhythm—like the Creed's saying that Jesus "rose *again*." Nothing is lost if it is omitted; it just smoothes the flow of language. The chief purpose in dealing with these variations here is to help the pupil accept variety in usage of the prayer without either feeling superior because he has the best version or uncomfortable because he might not be saying the right words.

You might ask pupils to turn to Matthew 6:13 in the Revised Standard Version for the footnote on the Doxology. The footnote (*n*) may deserve some explanation, since it refers to "other authorities, some ancient." Pupils may not realize that we have no original copy of Matthew and that the Bible had to be copied by hand for many, many centuries. If pupils themselves were to copy Matthew by hand, they would be sure to make some mistakes (imagine the added mistakes if someone else copied their copy). Moreover, the ancient scholars felt no wrong in adding extra words from time to time. If their worship practices added a doxology to Jesus' words, they would have felt perfectly free to insert the Doxology in the Gospel of Matthew. Whether this was what happened or not makes little difference—it might have happened that way, and the result carried over into the King James Version. Today we have discovered much older copies of Matthew than they had in King James' day, so the Revised Standard Version makes the Doxology a footnote.

"Two Records"

Ask the pupils to compare the two accounts of the Lord's Prayer in detail, noting the differences indicated in the pupil's book. Would they agree that Luke gives the proper setting and that Matthew combined the Lord's Prayer with Jesus' other teachings on prayer? Or do they feel that this prayer was given on two separate occasions? (There is no good reason why he wouldn't teach this prayer more than once.)

Since Luke 11:2–4 will not be considered further, some attention may be given to: (*a*) the common practice of each rabbi's giving his followers his own special set form of prayer; (*b*) the reference to John the Baptist, a reminder that some of Jesus' disciples had previously been followers of the Baptist; and (*c*) the fact that, although the disciples were already praying men, something in Jesus' prayer life was different, and they wanted it in their own prayer life.

"Structure"

Use the accounts in Matthew and Luke to structure the Lord's Prayer. Put the various parts side by side in columns (the pupils could do this in their Prayer Notebooks), somewhat as follows:

120

	Matthew	Luke
Introduction	Our Father who art in heaven,	Father,
First Petition	Hallowed be thy name.	hallowed be thy name.
Second Petition	Thy kingdom come,	Thy kingdom come.
Third Petition	Thy will be done, On earth as it is in heaven.	
Fourth Petition	Give us this day our daily bread;	Give us each day our daily bread;
Fifth Petition	And forgive us our debts, As we also have forgiven our debtors;	and forgive us our sins, for we ourselves forgive every one who is indebted to us;
Sixth Petition	And lead us not into temptation,	and lead us not into temptation.
Seventh Petition	But deliver us from evil.	

After these parallel columns have been set, attention might be given the following points:

a) *Omissions in Luke. Did he regard the Third and Seventh Petitions merely as rephrasings of previous petitions (as in Hebrew poetry where the second phrase of a Psalm often rewords the first)?*

b) *The usual division into four parts: introduction, "Thy" petitions, "Us" petitions, conclusion.*

c) *The use of three's and seven's (both regarded as symbolic numbers, the three standing for the Trinity, the seven for the Trinity plus the four points of the compass). If a popular grouping were observed, the three "Thy" petitions would be balanced by three "Us" petitions (combining the sixth and seventh). If the structure followed by Luther is examined, the seven petitions are retained.*

"The Model Prayer"

Modern advertising methods could be examined to distinguish between "needs" and "wants." Note how often television commercials or magazine ads appeal to popularity and recognition, to personal pleasures, to status. By appealing to these needs, they change what we merely want into what we think is absolutely necessary.

Reverse the order followed by advertising, and ask pupils how something they need becomes something they want. When someone says, "This is good for you," what do pupils think? That it is thereby unpleasant and distasteful? Does it have to be sugar-coated? Are we aware that we're asking out of need when we pray, "Hallowed be thy name"? Does the Lord's Prayer itself awaken needs we hadn't thought of? Is this one reason that this prayer is peculiar to Christians—that it asks for gifts non-Christians wouldn't think of asking for? Who except Christians would pray, "Thy kingdom come"? (Allow room for differences of opinion here. Your questions are to stimulate curiosity and thought, not to press for final answers here.)

You might also set this prayer against selfishness in prayer. Note how often prayer is self-directed rather than God-directed—based on what seems closest and most immediate to ourselves. We measure it by answers rather than by the delight of being heard.

Ask if prayers can get too selfish and personal. Can pupils cite examples? Can we possibly escape selfishness in prayer? Cite the Lord's Prayer as one which widens horizons, asks for gifts we wouldn't ordinarily seek, encompasses needs that may not occur to us, sees beyond the immediate needs to the last day, and unites each pray-er in a countless host. It's largely in this sense that it serves as a model.

Its use both at beginning and close of worship may be noted. In both instances, we say, "Lest I leave out things I should be praying for, I pray the words that cover all needs."

3. Have pupils work on their Prayer Notebooks.

Hymns that might be examined for the spirit of prayer include: "Behold us, Lord, a little space" (213); "Teach me, my God and King" (451); "Lord, teach us how to pray aright" (452); "Prayer is the soul's sincere desire" (458).

You might suggest one hymn as a starting point, letting pupils examine other hymns in that section of the hymnal for other illustrations. They can put these into their Prayer Notebooks after the session.

4. Have a memorization period.

This could be a period for group recital of sections to be memorized and for personal guidance of pupils who memorize with difficulty. Have those who memorize rapidly team up with those who are slower. If a degree of worship is sought, the section could be part of an affirmation of faith, prefaced by "I believe that . . ." ("I believe that God's name certainly is holy in itself, etc.") In succeeding sessions, pupils may also use this period to recite various memorized meanings.

5. Outline unit research projects.

List the topics with their datelines. If pupils are slow to volunteer, don't press them, but suggest how they might go about the project, offer resources for their use, and put your own assistance at their disposal.

6. Make assignments for the next session.

Have pupils study Chapter 19 and the Bible passages in the pupil's book.

---

session 19
SCOPE OF THE SESSION

Beginning with this session the Lord's Prayer is studied in slow motion. Implications of the simple words in the Introduction and First Petition come into view. Help pupils probe for deeper meanings in "Father" and "heaven" and "hallowed" and "name." The underlying petition is for reverence—in speech and attitude, as well as in all of life.

MATERIALS NEEDED

Bibles. *Service Book and Hymnal.* Prayer Notebooks. Pupil's book (Chapter 19).

AN OVERVIEW OF THE SESSION

1. *See Jesus' intention in giving the Lord's Prayer.*
2. *Review the various sections of Chapter 19 of the pupil's book.*
3. *Use Prayer Notebooks for rephrasing the First Petition and for copying hymns or hymn stanzas appropriate to hallowing God's name.*
4. *Make assignments for the next session.*

SESSION PLAN IN GREATER DETAIL

1. See Jesus' intention in giving The Lord's Prayer.

Refer to Matthew 5:5–6. Ask what Jesus meant, how his words tie in with the Lord's Prayer, whether he intended prayer to be private. Set this against the Jewish practice of making a show of praying, fasting, and almsgiving. Jesus' words are, therefore, directed at eliminating display as a motive for prayer. He urges his disciples to hide what they are inclined to show. He really exaggerates the privacy of prayer here—simply to get his point across.

2. Follow Chapter 19 of the pupil's book.

When pupils take part in a group recital of the Lord's Prayer, whom do they include in *"Our* Father"? The fifteen or twenty in the room? The hundred or more in public worship? The whole Christian church on earth? Even those who aren't joining in at the moment?

Ask if there is any such thing as private prayer. Doesn't a purely private prayer become selfish? Why do we persist in using "I" in confessing faith and "we" with prayer?

Your purpose here is to stretch pupils' minds to feel the link with the countless hosts of believers in prayer. Some attention may be given intercessory prayer—the sustaining power felt by persons prayed for; the spiritual link between persons hundreds of miles apart who are joined in common prayer. No need to analyze how this can be; merely indicate it as the witness of believers.

"Father"

Ask pupils to examine the forms of address used in collects, prayer hymns, etc. Are they at variance with "Father"? Or do they imply "Father"?

Leviticus 22:1–3 provides a sample of setting things or people apart, and, therefore, giving them special respect. This passage could apply to coming to church with a dirty face or sloppy clothes, suggesting how clothes and appearance reveal respect and honor for "Our Father." (This is not the same thing as saying that antiseptic hands and dressy clothes are requirements for worship.)

Salutations used in letters might be considered. What forms of address are used—in business letters, circulars, love letters, letters to your family? Are they merely forms, or do they mean something more? Note how love letters between a couple may change over the years, beginning with rather formal salutations and gradually using more and more terms that suggest an endearing relationship. Then note the difference between addressing God as "the Eternal" or "the Almighty" and as "Father."

You may tie this study in quite properly with the relationship confessed in the First Article of the Creed, and with the idea of prayers as a relationship. If pupils were to think of God as a "cosmic urge," what difference would it make in their praying? If their address were "O angel spirits," would it make any difference? If they began, "If there be a God . . . ," would it make any difference?

"In Heaven"

How would pupils define heaven? As a place? A state of being? Outer space? Wherever God is?

You might elaborate on figures of speech discussed in the pupil's book—like the use of "up" for heaven. We carry terms of altitude and elevation into many areas—going "up" the ladder of success, being "above" a scheming plan. We speak of one thing as "low-down," another as "uplifting." Thus, heaven is "up" and often thought of in terms of the sky. So long as this is regarded as a figure of speech and not a literal place, no harm is done. As the heavens are high above the earth, so are God's ways higher than man's.

Your emphasis here, however, is to underscore reverence in approaching God. Draw the contrast with Tin Pan Alley names for God—like "the man upstairs" or a "co-pilot"—that border on the profane. "In heaven" keeps us at a respectful distance, avoiding chumminess. God is approached cheerfully and confidently, yet with awesome reverence.

"Set Apart"

You might ask if pupils have things at home that are "taboo"—things that can't be touched or peeked at, things set aside for special use. Sunday clothes might come into this category, to be worn only on dress-up occasions.

Expand this to include things set apart in church—the area around the altar, for example. It's reserved for those charged with the conduct of worship or those having special business there (like altar guild or acolyte). The church sanctuary itself might be cited, indicating the need for propriety of activities and demeanor there.

Such illustrations will show how things come to be hallowed. You can then move from these examples to "What's in a Name?" and consider the hallowing of God's name.

"What's in a Name?"

While the Second Commandment will not be studied in detail until next year, its link with the First Petition is intentional. What do pupils regard as included in that commandment? Does it apply to swear words, or does it go beyond them? To what can we rightfully attach God's name? Does it apply to more than speech? Or does speech reflect respect and disrespect? Do we shrink from cursing because the words are bad, or because we hold God's name in such reverence? The passages from Matthew 5 and Ephesians refer to reverence for God's name in speech and life respectively.

The tie with baptism is implied here, since in baptism we become bearers of God's name. Like a family name, we bear it throughout our life, honoring it or dishonoring it. Luther's explanation shows how far beyond speech the First Petition goes: "anyone who teaches or lives contrary to the Word of God dishonors God's name among us." The First Petition embraces all of life.

The passages from Exodus, Genesis, and Matthew 1 all consider the meaning of a name. Note the significance given a name in each instance. The Exodus passage is especially important. Ask pupils why God should call himself "I AM." Does it suggest that if everything dissolved God would still exist? Does it also suggest that everything is present with God? That, like a circle, he has neither beginning nor ending, neither past nor future?

In summarizing this discussion, center pupils' attention on reverence and respect as the dominant attitudes of the First Petition. Refer to postures indicative of respect—bowing before a king, kneeling for confession, tipping the hat, even seating arrangements at public functions. All are marks of respect.

For a moment contrast respect with disrespect and cynicism, where little is held sacred, where belittling and discrediting are widely practiced. The First Petition places the pray-ers on the side of those who hold certain things in honor—things linked with the name and will of God.

If you want to anticipate the Ten Commandments further at this point, you might allude to them as the list of respects or reverences for life. They are the things or persons God wants us to hold in honor—his name, his word and house, his parents and rightful superiors, human life, marriage, others' property and their good name and rights. Behind each commandment lies an emphasis on reverence.

3. Work on the Prayer Notebooks.

The introduction to Unit D suggests prayer hymns suitable for inclusion in the Prayer Notebooks. Pupils may also scan such hymns as "Jesus, Name of wondrous love" (SBH 50) and "All hail the power of Jesus' Name" (SBH 426). Your timetable will govern time allotted to this in the session itself. If you are pressed for time, ask pupils to continue their work on the Prayer Notebooks at home. Ask that they bring their notebooks to class sessions.

4. Make assignments for the next session.

Assign Chapter 20 and the Bible passages for study.

If you feel that memorizing should be done at home rather than during session time, make it a homework assignment. However, allow time in the session for pupils to repeat memorized portions.

The research project for next week is on the "kingdom of God." If a pupil has accepted this assignment, alert him to his deadline, reminding other research pupils of their deadlines.

---

session 20
SCOPE OF THE SESSION

The Second Petition of the Lord's Prayer combines present and future. It focuses on both the coming of God's kingdom to us day by day and the unrealized coming of his kingdom at the last day. It also poses the dilemma between the kingdom of this world and the kingdom of Christ. It stands as the most visionary petition of the Lord's Prayer.

This session will consider various facets of the "kingdom of God": as a society; as God's rule over all life; as present possession and future hope; as the result of God's work alone. If you find the study of the Second and Third Petitions running together and seeming to overlap, no harm is done; the two petitions may be regarded as having no fixed boundary between them.

MATERIALS NEEDED

Bibles. Copies of the *Service Book and Hymnal*. Prayer Notebooks. Pupil's book (Chapter 20).

AN OVERVIEW OF THE SESSION

1. Ask the pupils for their ideas of a model home.
2. Discuss why we keep on praying for the kingdom of God.
3. Have pupil reports and Bible study on Jesus' teaching about the "kingdom."
4. Use sections of pupil's book on "God's Kingship," "Two Directions," "Two Ways God Rules," and "Company" to draw some conclusions from Jesus' teaching.
5. Using Prayer Notebooks, ask pupils to add prayer hymns that echo the Second Petition.
6. Make assignments for the next session.

SESSION PLAN IN GREATER DETAIL

1. Ask pupils for their idea of a model home.

Because pupils may have a fuzzy idea of "a perfect society," the home is suggested as a social unit to bring the whole subject within range.

Ask how pupils would achieve a model home. Would they do it by pooling goods so that nothing belonged to any one person exclusively? By having money to get all the conveniences? By appliances and swimming pools? By allowing each person to go his own way, to have all he wants, to do what he wants? Do they think of a perfect home only in material terms? Would they surround their home with love, respect, faithfulness, fair play, sacrifice?

Since people are always imperfect, can there ever be a perfect home? Are there moments when a home can be near perfection—perhaps during a family crisis that draws a family closer together? What changes would pupils like to make in their own homes?

Allow adequate time for this discussion, since the points discussed here can be related closely to the larger society of God's kingdom. For example, pupils may feel they have "a taste" of a perfect home now and then (just as they have "a taste" of the kingdom of God—a kind of present possession), but its fulfillment will elude them (just as the kingdom of God is future too). Moreover, help the pupils see the importance of spiritual qualities in the home now (just as the kingdom of God implies God's kingship not only in name but also in fact over all of life now).

2. Discuss why we pray for the kingdom of God.

An examination of Luther's explanation of the Second Petition is appropriate here. Despite the hopelessness of bringing the kingdom to pass, Christians can't help but labor for its coming, regardless of setbacks or seeming futility. (Refer to "The Endless Prayer" in the pupil's book.)

You might liken the Christian's perseverance to that of plants which are plowed under but persist in shooting stalks upward. Compare it to the work of Christian missions cut off from the mother churches by an Iron or Bamboo Curtain. These missions are always ready to spring back to life, regardless of losses.

At this point, too, you may want to discuss the limits of our prayers—whether we should limit our petitions to what we can reasonably expect to get, or whether we dare pray for the impossible. John 16:23 might be studied here.

3. Hear pupils' reports and explore Bible passages.

If a pupil has volunteered to report on Jesus' teaching on the kingdom of God, allow time for his report. Discuss its salient points. Then move to the Bible passages for further analysis of Jesus' teaching.

The passages present a mixture of teachings. Some apply to the future exclusively, others to the present. Ask pupils to note the absence of reference to man's bringing the kingdom to pass.

Three of the passages, Matthew 22:1–10, 25:1–13, and 1 Thessalonians 5:1–11, may be deferred until the next step, since they apply in part to the second coming of Christ. In the other passages, ask pupils to look for what each says about the kingdom of God. Matthew 13:24–30 may be presented as a picture of the church today—a mixture of good and bad, redeemed and unredeemed—and what to do about it.

Matthew 3:17 may merit deeper study, as it indicates the dawn of God's kingdom in the coming of Christ. In Christ God's love reaches its fullest expression, ushering in a new age. Thus, when a believer comes under the kingship of Christ, he is a new creation; the kingdom of God has come to him. (This passage may be cited when "Two Directions" is studied, as it gives a *past* tense to the kingdom. Thus, the kingdom of God has come in Christ, comes now to the believer, and will come at the last day.)

The dating of the coming kingdom may deserve some attention, especially if pupils are exposed to religious groups bent on such cryptic dating. The misfires in Christian history such as the Millerites might be noted—also the appeal to fear (as compared with the joy Jesus emphasized)—and the necessity of establishing a date reasonably soon (who would be interested in a date two centuries away?). Passages from Matthew 25 and 1 Thessalonians 5 are especially apt here. Also Matthew 22, with its banquet figure.

God's activity in bringing about his kingdom likewise deserves strong emphasis. One could almost say that his kingdom comes *in spite of* man, not through man's efforts. Man's efforts end in a tower of Babel, not in a holy city from heaven. Luke 11:14–20 may be read hastily here—not to suggest a blueprint for the kingdom, but to underscore the fact that man cannot bring it about.

4. Discuss other material in Chapter 20.

Drawing on the pupil's report, the Bible passages, and the remaining sections of the pupil's book, ask pupils to assemble their findings on the kingdom of God. These may be listed on a chalkboard as pupils suggest them.

The section "Two Ways God Rules" in the pupil's book weighs the dilemma of all Christians—that of living under two kingdoms at the same time. We simply have to live with it as the seat of the struggle of the Christian life. Make the point: We are *in* the world, but *not of* the world.

Luther's insights about the two separate kingdoms are worth exploring: God is the ruler of both the kingdom of the world and God's kingdom to come. Christ is the lord of both kingdoms. The kingdom of the world, however, is ruled by law, by force, since it does not have the gospel. The Christian must live in this world even though he lives under God's kingdom, too.

Some attention might be given to this tension. Christ calls us to be Christian wherever we are, whether in business or school or politics or in the home, to take our Christianity into every area of the kingdom of the world. No area of life is beyond the concern of the gospel. One cannot put religion into a pigeonhole and divorce it from all other areas of living. If the church has no concern for politics or economics, it ceases to touch people in their daily concerns.

5. Have pupils work on their Prayer Notebooks.

Have the class use hymnals to seek prayer hymns that echo the

Second Petition. (See the introduction to Unit D for suggestions.) Ask pupils to include also a rephrasing of this petition.

6. Make assignments for the next session.

Assign Chapter 21 in the pupil's book and whatever memorization you have decided is necessary.

Check with pupils who have research reports due next week.

---

session 21
SCOPE OF SESSION

The Third Petition of the Lord's Prayer, omitted by Luke, may be a rephrasing of the Second Petition. God's kingdom comes when his will is done. This session, therefore, could be closely linked with the previous one. Reread the article "Prayer and the Lord's Prayer" to maintain your perspective.

The pupil's book considers the problem of reconciling suffering with the will of God. This problem was considered in the previous term. There it was viewed in its bearing on faith; here its bearing on prayer is considered.

You may feel that undue emphasis is given this problem. Luther makes no reference to it in his explanation, so why should we? Help the pupils to understand that the will of God does not order suffering and evil, that God wills only our well-being, our loyalty and trust in time of trouble, and our eternal life with him. Stress the "good and gracious will of God."

Two premises underlie the treatment suggested here: (1) that people generally think of tragedy and suffering when you mention God's will to them; (2) that people generally try to distinguish between the "will of God" (which they regard as impersonal and arbitrary) and the "will of Jesus Christ."

We suggest that the problem be explored carefully; and that, after discussing possible solutions, you describe the will of God as something "good and gracious," asking pupils to view it as they view the will of Jesus Christ.

MATERIALS NEEDED

Bibles. Copies of the *Service Book and Hymnal*. Prayer Notebooks. Newspaper and magazine clippings of tragedy or suffering. Pupil's book (Chapter 21).

AN OVERVIEW OF THE SESSION

1. *Discuss human reactions to the problem of suffering.*
2. *See the relationship between the Book of Job and Jesus' prayer at Gethsemane.*

3. *Explore Bible passages dealing with God's will.*
4. *Examine ways we may know God's will for us.*
5. *Have pupils work on their Prayer Notebooks.*
6. *Have a period for memorizing Luther's explanation of the Third Petition.*
7. *Make assignments for the next session.*

SESSION PLAN IN GREATER DETAIL
1. Discuss possible reactions to suffering.

Use newspaper and magazine clippings of disasters to provoke discussion. You may also cite local instances of tragedy or suffering, e.g. floods, fires, storms. After each ask what the will of God has to do with this. How can pupils reconcile the will of a loving, all-powerful God to what happens to people?

If a pupil has prepared a report on fatalism, this might be used as a springboard to open up the problem and suggest some possible answers. Proceed beyond the pupil's report with a consideration of the first five sections of Chapter 21 of the pupil's book.

Three frequent answers are indicated in the pupil's book (see sections entitled "Fatalism," "Spartans," and "What God Permits"). The first two try to accept things as they are without accounting for them— "That's the way the ball bounces." Both are sometimes regarded as Christian points of view and marks of faith. Both provide a possible, if unhappy, way of meeting misfortune.

You might have the pupils consider the appeal of fatalism and Spartanism for a moment. A soldier fights more bravely if he feels that some unseen destiny rules the battlefield—or does he? If a piece of shrapnel has his number, he can do nothing about it; so why worry? One soldier can go through battle without a scar, another is killed on the first volley. Is one a saint and the other a sinner? Does one have a medal? Was one meant to be spared?

The Spartans made idols of bravery and courage—much like the American Indians with their contempt for weakness and their admiration for a gauntlet-runner. Here again they viewed life as governed by a mysterious force. They toughened themselves up; one misfortune only served to muscle them for the next. Is such courage Christian? (Compare this view with Paul's view in 2 Corinthians 12 where he boasts of his weakness as the vehicle for God's strength.)

The third answer is probably more satisfying to a Christian. Here a distinction is drawn between God's decree and what he permits. This view allows for the "good and gracious will of God" despite the misfortunes and tragedies of life. If suffering comes, it isn't because God necessarily decrees it. He simply allows it as a part of human life—the very nature of things. Luther points out that God's will is directed to strengthening us in our faith and keeping us close to him all our lives. Have the pupils take a close look at Luther's explanation.

Ask pupils which view offers a satisfying answer? Or are all still wrapped in enigma?

2. Link the Book of Job with Jesus' prayer at Gethsemane.

Have the pupil's report on the Book of Job. If no one accepted this research responsibility, you could ask pupils what they know about this book of the Bible. Be sure to check the details yourself in a Bible dictionary. This is important enough to become a major learning experience in this session. Take as much time as you need. What do they know about Job? What is his story? What arguments are summoned by Job's friends? What is Job's reaction to these arguments? If these questions are met by blank stares, ask pupils to read Job 1—2 hastily for the plot. Then outline briefly the arguments of Job's friends—mainly (a) that suffering is a result of sin, either known or unknown, (b) that the wicked may seem to escape, but the sin will soon find them out, (c) that pain chastens and suffering builds character. Then move from there to the resolution of Job's problems.

Job never found the answer to his question, but he found something more—that God had not forsaken him. Actually Job wanted more than an answer; he wanted some reassurance that God cared for him even in the midst of all his trouble.

You might ask pupils which is really more important—to have a nice, pat explanation for the problem, or to have spiritual power to see a misfortune through? Do people really want to know "why" or do they want a power to fill their weakness? Instead of "Why did this happen?" help them to see that the real question is, "What am I to do about it now?" One of the most important learnings of this session is that God's will for us is demonstrated by the fact that his love surrounds us in the midst of trial and misfortune. Help your pupils develop this Christian attitude toward suffering and tragedy.

The Gethsemane prayer should be probed for its underlying spirit. Ask if pupils think the cross could have been avoided. Love made it necessary, not the forces of circumstance or the deepening of a plot. Thus, Gethsemane is a far cry from fatalism or Spartanism. It is an example of submission to the divine will, but it is a joyful submission and a renewal of strength to see it through.

3. Explore Bible passages.

Luke 22:39-46 and Isaiah 55:6-9 ("My thoughts are not your thoughts") could be linked to the study of Gethsemane; the John 9:1-4 passage to the three answers given above. Note in the latter passage how Jesus seems to evade the question (certainly he doesn't answer it), and turns their attention to "What now?" How much comfort would a blind man get merely to know what caused his blindness? How much more comfort to have a power to see it through?

1 Peter 2:21-25 sets the problem of suffering squarely where it belongs. Any answer must square up with the suffering of Jesus. His innocence was without parallel, yet he suffered. Why? If the sufferer knows nothing else, he knows he is in company with Jesus himself!

1 John 4:7-12 can mark the swing of the pendulum in this session —from considering the will of God and suffering to considering the "good and gracious" will of God. This might be the time to raise ques-

tions about identifying the will of God with that of Jesus. Do pupils have different mental pictures for each? Should they be different? Isn't the will of God really the will we see in Christ?

1 John 5:1–5 follows this idea and sees obedience as a mark of love, not of painful duty. Can a person obey because he wants to, not because he *has* to? Can pupils cite instances of this—where the relationship of trust is so strong that one would fear to hurt a loved one, or that he would anticipate a loved one's will, and obey?

4. Examine ways we may know God's will for us.

If no report is given, a summary statement of the petition would be in order. God's will is known through his acts—even as ours is known through our speech and deeds. And it is revealed supremely in Jesus Christ; by him it must always be measured.

The two emphases in this petition might be described as submission to a loving Father who knows and does best for us, and trust in a Father who stands by us no matter what we face.

Marginal attention might be given here to "on earth as it is in heaven." It could lead pupils far afield into the mysterious world of angels. For your purposes, angels may be regarded as God's agents for the accomplishing of his purposes. The completeness of God's reign in heaven thus becomes the goal of this petition—that it may come on earth too, in spite of every obstacle.

5. Have pupils work on their Prayer Notebooks.

Several things may be included here: (*a*) rephrasing of the Third Petition, (*b*) prayers of the pupil's own composition for use in opening and closing sessions, (*c*) prayers of "commendation." The prayers of "commendation" can be found among evening prayer hymns or evening prayers. The dominant thought is that of entrusting all we are and have into God's hands.

6. Have a memorizing period.

Since you may find time pressing, this activity may be edged into homework, with provision made for checking during the next session.

7. Make assignments for the next session.

Ask pupils to read Chapter 22 in the pupil's book. Alert students who have reports due at the next session.

---

session 22
SCOPE OF SESSION

Chapter 22 of the pupil's book sets the emphases of this session dealing with the Fourth Petition of the Lord's Prayer. Several points are underscored there: (1) the inclusion of the hungry in this petition; (2) the note of thanksgiving; (3) the emphasis on trust for daily needs; and (4) the warning against hoarding at the expense of others.

Luther's explanation of this petition is central here. He includes under "daily bread" all things necessary to bodily life and sets the dominant motif as that of thanksgiving.

Since this session introduces the "Us" petitions, attention may be given in passing to the over-all character of these petitions. Each one has a forceful verb ("give," "forgive," "lead," "deliver"), in contrast to the "Thy" petitions, which have verbs that are almost passive. (After each "Thy" petition, the pray-er may ask "by whom?")

MATERIALS NEEDED

Bibles. Copies of the *Service Book and Hymnal*. Prayer Notebooks. News items on efforts to feed the hungry and on welfare programs. Bible dictionary. Pupil's book (Chapter 22).

AN OVERVIEW OF THE SESSION

1. Find out which petition pupils think the most practical.
2. Use Chapter 22 of the pupil's book as a guide and starting point for discussion. If a pupil has prepared a report on "Why Pray for We Can't Have?" have it here.
3. Ask pupils as a group to rephrase the Fourth Petition, placing their new version in their Prayer Notebooks.
4. Have pupils look for prayer hymns and collects that illustrate the Fourth Petition and copy them in their Prayer Notebooks.
5. If there is time, check on memory work.
6. Make assignments for the next session.

SESSION PLAN IN GREATER DETAIL

1. Ask pupils which petition is most practical.

Begin by asking which commandment pupils regard as most important. Follow by asking which petition they consider most practical.

Pupils will probably cite the commandment on killing as most important. Laws of society make it a capital offense, and no such punishment is legislated for violations of other commandments. However, you may note that four commandments precede this one, and the commandments are given in a descending order of importance.

The same feeling might prevail for the petitions of the Lord's Prayer. Pupils may feel that "Thy" petitions are largely a build-up for the petition for daily bread. While no priority can be seen among the petitions, each petition has an importance of its own. However, the prayers for reverence and God's kingdom and submission involve needs that often have to be awakened, while "daily bread" is an everyday need.

Matthew 6:25-33 may be examined on this point. It indicates that worry about daily bread is God's business (he knows our needs), while worry about his kingdom should be our business.

2. Follow the presentation of material in Chapter 22 of the pupil's book.

The various meanings of "bread" are suggested in the pupil's book. You might probe them deeper by asking what bread means to a baker whose livelihood depends on it; to Jean Valjean in Victor Hugo's *Les Miserables*, who was sent to the French galleys for having stolen a loaf; to a communicant at the altar; to a junior high school student who takes his lunch, but finds no bread for sandwiches. Such values will help pupils see beyond the wrapped loaf.

You might also examine Luther's catalogue for "daily bread." Does he include too much? What do weather, good name, neighbors have to do with this petition?

Some attention might be given a broader topic here, such as the way God not only creates hungers, but also provides for them. The appetites of the body—not just for food, but for love and marriage—are God-given. It would not be foreign to this petition to suggest sex as God-given. There's nothing evil about sex, however it may be abused. Hunger for food can lead to gluttony—also an abuse of something God-given. God would be cruel to give men hungers and then make sport of them by not providing for their satisfaction.

Some discussion might center on God's concern for bodily needs. Can a person be divided up, as though one part were body and another spirit? How can you split a personality? Is God more concerned with spirit than with body? Are those people right who try to spiritualize "bread" and make it apply to the "bread of life"?

The John 6:27–35 passage and Exodus 16:13–21 should be considered in this context. Ask pupils what Jesus meant by calling himself "the bread of life." (He was referring to his own life as being necessary for the eternal life of every person.) Is this what we mean by daily bread? Has Luther missed the point in failing to spiritualize bread?

Exodus 16 alludes to the manna in the wilderness. Have pupils note that it was provided; it could not be hoarded. The Israelites did nothing but collect it for their needs day by day. Check a Bible dictionary for details. How would this apply to God's provision for daily needs today?

"Day by Day"

Note that this petition is corporate, not private. Who is included here? Would a pray-er include starving humanity? And would he see himself as part of God's means of alleviating the hungers of others?

A good discussion question is: If the lands and deposits of earth produce more than enough to feed all of life, why do so many people go hungry? Is it right to hoard food while others starve? How can this problem be eased? (A big part of the problem lies in distribution—how to get foods where they are needed most. Another part is the regard for bread as a weapon—the bartering of resources for friendship and loyalty.)

"For the Birds"

Passages from Matthew 6, 2 Thessalonians 3:6–10, and 1 Timothy 6:6–10 may be studied in connection with this and the following sections. Since the heart of God's provision for daily needs is seen in Matthew 6, closer scrutiny would be helpful. Is God's provision for birds an apt analogy to his provision for man? Amateur ornithologists may have some observations on the ways birds get their food.

Out of this may emerge a discussion about the Christian's provision for the future. Does it show a lack of trust to invest in life insurance, pension programs, social security, etc.? Should we live on a hand-to-mouth basis, like the birds? (Some birds, however, do make future provision, as when they store sunflower seeds in the rough bark of a tree.)

"With Thanksgiving"

The pupil's report may be used here to launch this section. If no report has been prepared, ask what difference praying makes in our "daily bread." Would we have less if we didn't pray? Is this petition meant to keep us on the good side of God, just in case? How does praying bring daily bread? How does it bring health or prosperity or other material benefits?

Such a discussion may backtrack to the deeper meaning of prayer, in terms of relationship with God—praying for our human needs that we may continue to serve him. It may also broaden the scope of the petition to include anything pertaining to our bodily life. Even the incurably sick can pray to be made whole. Even the starving, with no hope of food in sight, can ask for bread.

In this connection you might ask if pupils could improve on God's way of handling our daily needs. If he were really fair, wouldn't he see to it that special material favors came to believers? Wouldn't he divide up this world's goods more evenly?

You might also allude here to answers to prayer (a subject not seriously dealt with heretofore). Must some kind of trademark appear, like "Made in Heaven," to give God credit or show proof that he is answering prayer? Material needs can be provided in quite natural ways. Where then does God or prayer fit in? The wicked are fed quite as much as the upright. What difference, then, if you pray or don't pray?

In probing this area, ask if things are any less an answer to prayer when they come in natural ways. Must they defy all known laws and bear the stamp of the miraculous? Is the supernatural at odds with the natural? Must the one be discredited for the other to stand out? (Note how people feel they must belittle medicine in order to exalt faith as a healing power. Can't the two go hand in hand?)

Study the passages from Psalm 103:1–5 and Proverbs 15:17, 17:1. Part of Psalm 103 may be inserted in the Prayer Notebook. Instances of the truth of Proverbs may be cited by pupils—tension at meals, for example, when family members stalk away no longer hungry because of emotional upset. Luther's catalogue under "daily bread" might be examined in the light of these verses from Proverbs.

3. Have the class rephrase the petition.

If thanksgiving is at the heart of this petition, a list of things to be thankful for might provide a starter. In addition to "Give us," pupils may want to include "We thank thee" items.

4. Have pupils work on their Prayer Notebooks.

Have pupils look for prayer hymns and collects illustrating the Fourth Petition and copy them in Prayer Notebooks. Ask pupils to think of expressing each petition in a single word, associating terms like "reverence" and "thanksgiving" with the parts of the Lord's Prayer. Then have them rephrase this petition in their own words.

Table graces (either copied or of the pupils' own phrasing) could be added to the Prayer Notebooks; also the rephrasing of the Fourth Petition.

Associating key words with various petitions of the Lord's Prayer hasn't been attempted to date. Ask pupils what single word could gather up the heart of each petition. The four petitions studied thus far may be written, with the following words (or suitable synonyms) opposite the respective petitions; reverence, hope, submission, and thanksgiving.

5. Have a memorization period.

You may ask for oral recitations here (or group recitations if the class is large) or use some other method for checking memory progress. Ask pupils to learn Luther's explanation of the Fourth Petition. An exact knowledge of the wording of the explanation of "daily bread" isn't necessary, but pupils should know the general ideas.

6. Make assignments for the next session.

Ask pupils to read Chapter 23 and the Bible passages. Check on pupils who will report on "Jesus' Teaching About Forgiveness." Assign memorization of the Fifth Petition.

---

session 23
SCOPE OF SESSION

Forgiveness is so common a term in Christian conversation that it is sometimes threadbare of meaning. If you succeed in bringing home to your pupils the meaning of forgiveness in terms of *healing a broken relationship,* you will have accomplished much in this session.

Much of Chapter 23 of the pupil's book deals with the various meanings of "trespasses" in the New Testament. This is not merely to explain the interchange of "debts" and "trespasses" in the Fifth Petition, but to indicate ways by which the relationship with God is broken. You may define sin as "being or doing other than God wants us to be or do"; but set it against the relationship of a loving Father.

In approaching this session and in conducting it, keep central Jesus' Parable of the Unmerciful Servant (Matthew 18:23–25) which, despite its negative emphasis, provides the central theme.

MATERIALS NEEDED

Bibles. Copies of the *Service Book and Hymnal.* Prayer Notebooks. Bible dictionary. Concordance. Pupil's book (Chapter 23).

AN OVERVIEW OF THE SESSION

1. Involve pupils in a discussion of forgiveness and seeking forgiveness.

2. Discuss the relationship of wrongs and punishments.

3. Extend this discussion to the Old Testament view of sacrifice.

4. Consider the various meanings of "sin," using Bible passages with appropriate sections of Chapter 23. Have the pupil's report on "Jesus' Teaching About Forgiveness."

5. Have pupils rephrase the Fifth Petition, using Luther's explanation as a guide.

6. Make assignments for the next session.

SESSION PLAN IN GREATER DETAIL

1. Use a current problem to provoke a discussion of forgiveness.

Examples might be drawn from political clashes, international disputes, school fights, auto accidents involving innocent bystanders. Try to cite a case in which one side seems to have a more legitimate grievance.

The example should lead to such questions as: How far should a person go in forgiving? Does it depend on the seriousness of the offense? If someone bumps you accidentally, is that the same as if it were done deliberately—so far as forgiveness goes? Are there some things you just can't forgive? Why? How much does personal honor enter into the picture? Rivalry? Humiliation? Which is more embarrassing—to seek forgiveness or to forgive?

You may turn the spotlight of such questions on the local example you have cited. If it is a group or national example, you could also ask if groups or nations can ever really forgive. Aren't they basically interested in preserving their own honor, or "face"?

Your purpose here is not to solve a grievance question, but to help pupils feel the urgency, sharpness, and timeliness of forgiveness in real situations.

2. Discuss the relationship between wrongs and punishments.

This step in the session plan and the next are closely connected. Examine both steps together to see their bearing on the Fifth Petition.

Several purposes lie behind this discussion: (1) to help pupils see how an offense against fellow men is also an offense against God; (2) to underscore the idea of forgiveness as a broken relationship, and of sacrifice as a means of restoring that relationship; (3) to illustrate the degrees of cost tailored to the offenses—"punishment fitting the crime"; and (4) to help the pupil understand his need of asking God's forgiveness for attitudes or actions that break his relationship with his heavenly Father.

Human societies are as strong as their laws and the enforcement of those laws. If people can get away with lawlessness, society soon breaks down. Thus, people establish laws and penalties for their common protection. If a man disobeys, he must be punished before he can be restored to the good graces of society.

While this may seem academic to a seventh-grader, you might illustrate it by asking what the penalties would be for parking overtime, for petty theft, for kidnaping, for murder. Why is one penalty greater than another? The Bible speaks of an "eye for an eye and a tooth for a tooth." Is the same idea that is behind such a Bible code also behind our penal system?

If pupils show an interest in this approach, you might go further by asking why criminal cases are entitled "The State [in Canada "The Crown"] versus John Doe." Why "the state"? "The Crown"? Has the state or Crown been injured? Does the term itself indicate a broken relationship—as though John Doe had been unfaithful to the trust his fellow citizens had in him?

3. Explore the view of sacrifice given in Leviticus 6:1–7.

The whole idea of sacrifice may be briefly discussed before entering on a study of Leviticus 6. You may deal with ways we "make up" to friends and neighbors for slights and offenses. Stress the idea that the greater the offense, the costlier the sacrifice required to make things right. We can pardon minor offenses, but find trouble forgiving something really major.

Leviticus 6:1–7—the ram without blemish offered as a guilt-offering for robbery—provides an Old Testament example of a blood sacrifice. Pupils may be familiar with other types of Old Testament sacrifice—cereal or grain, pigeons or turtledoves, sheep. (The incident of Jesus' cleansing of the Temple may be cited here. Pigeons and lambs and rams were sold there for sacrifice, a convenience to worshipers who could hardly manage to bring a lamb scores of miles.) Ask how pupils would rate the different sacrificial offerings. Which would be appropriate to the most serious offense? Which to the least serious? Go on to ask why blood was regarded as the mark of sacrifice. (It stood for life itself, the most precious of all possessions.) Why is Jesus referred to as the "Lamb of God"?

138

4. Consider various meanings of sin.

Note that three of the five terms for sin given in Chapter 23 apply to the "milder" forms of sin, as opposed to deliberate crime. The very mildness of "slipping across" or "debts" may be misleading, since both can be incurred without deliberate intent. You may want pupils to examine Luke 16:19–31 closely on this point (in connection with "slipping across"); ask if the punishment of the rich man isn't considerably out of line with his offense. Before the law one can scarcely be punished for what one doesn't do. Pupils may have difficulty accepting the seriousness of such an offense, but you can rest your case on the word of Jesus. In dealing with this material, try to draw out salient points so you can help the pupils summarize the discussion later.

Bible passages should be incorporated in the following pattern: Romans 13:8–10 and Galatians 6:1–5 into your discussion of "Debts"; Matthew 18:23–35 and Matthew 6:14–15 into your discussion of "Tit for Tat" and Romans 14:10–13 into your discussion of "Clean Confession."

Bible passages from Matthew 5 and 18 could be used on the subject of patching up differences. Pupils may note that Matthew 18:15–17 is embodied in many church constitutions as a procedure for patching up differences or exerting discipline. The bearing of these passages on the several sections of Chapter 23 should be sought.

It is important to help the pupils summarize the learnings of the session. The summary statement should follow the pupil's report on Jesus' teaching on forgiveness. If no report has been prepared, help the pupils formulate the summary on the chalkboard. If you feel that your group needs more time to consider the meaning of forgiveness, carry it over into the next session.

5. Have pupils rephrase the Fifth Petition.

As the pupils try to rephrase the Fifth Petition help them consider Luther's explanation. Ask what forgiveness has to do with praying. Why does Luther say "refuse to hear our prayer"? Could pupils cite a family quarrel that blocks communication between members of the family? Would this be what Luther meant?

Also, give some attention to "sin every day." Do pupils feel that once we're forgiven we're always forgiven? Can they see any possible link between this and the frequent receiving of the Lord's Supper? (Anticipate the study of the sacrament by referring to it as the seal of God's forgiveness—an assurance of his pardon.)

Pupils should note how Luther has restated the petition—not expressly as a prayer. Can they use Luther's explanation to put the petition into prayer form? Have them enter their rephrased prayers in their Prayer Notebook. Prayer hymns and collects appropriate to this petition could also be added.

6. Make assignments for the next session.

Ask pupils to read Chapter 24 and to be able to explain in their own words what "temptation" means.

session 24
SCOPE OF THE SESSION

If you have been proceeding on a session-by-session plan, you will be faced by a mountainous task in this session. It not only treats two practical petitions and the Doxology of the Lord's Prayer, but also should provide a period of review.

Chapter 24 of the pupil's book has twice as much material on the Sixth Petition as it has on the Seventh and the Doxology. This is because the Seventh Petition is viewed as a rephrasing of the essential meaning of the Sixth. You may weigh your own treatment according to the needs and interests of your group.

Since three of Luther's explanations are involved here, you may limit the memorizing to the Sixth Petition, reserving the other two for the next unit — unless your pupils have set a faster pace than is anticipated.

MATERIALS NEEDED

Pupil's book (Chapter 24). Bibles. Copies of the *Service Book and Hymnal*. Prayer Notebook.

AN OVERVIEW OF THE SESSION

1. Examine Jesus' meaning of the word "temptation."
2. Follow Chapter 24 of the pupil's book section by section. Have the pupil's report on "The Devil in the Bible."
3. Have pupils work on their Prayer Notebooks.
4. Set aside as review period to pull the whole unit together.
5. Conclude the unit, checking on memorization and asking for a brief evaluation from the pulpils.
6. Make assignments for the next session.

SESSION PLAN IN GREATER DETAIL

1. Probe what Jesus meant by "temptation."

Your purpose here is to pose the questions behind Chapter 24: whether temptation itself is to be avoided; whether the emphasis should be on being spared or on being strengthened. Let pupils substitute "testing" for "temptation" and see how it sounds.

2. Use Chapter 24 of pupil's book.

The first three Bible passages may be used with the first five sections; the next three passages with the "The Great Deceiver" and "Deliver"; and the final passage with "Doxology, For Thine Is . . . ." Each passage may be studied for its bearing on the section involved.

In addition, you may want to cite Matthew 4:1–11 and 1 Corinthians 10:13 for the section "Strengthen Us in Temptation."

140

While you will not dwell too long on any section, examine any questions that occur to you or to pupils on reading the sections. For example, you may want to discuss the risks of getting in with the wrong crowd under "Keep Us Out of Temptation"; or whether Jesus could be really tempted, as indicated in Matthew 4; or whether pupils are more sharply tempted by right versus wrong or by better versus good.

Under "Sources" you may weigh temptations coming from: (a) trying to make a favorable impression; (b) a weak spot within us; (c) a strong point within us that makes us think we're invulnerable; (d) well-meaning friends. Can pupils cite some examples? What temptations do they consider most trying? (To hold their tongue? To keep their eyes where they belong? To do what they know they should do?)

Some ways of dealing with temptations might be discussed under "Back to 'Our Father.'" What strengthens people when they are tried? How about their self-respect and good name? People who count on them? Traditions? Prayer? The presence of Christ?

Set the stage for a discussion of "The Great Deceiver" by asking if pupils believe in the Devil. How would they describe him? Or would they refer to his as "it"? What signs can be found for his existence and work? (If you had a report on "The Devil in the Bible" in the first term, you may refer to findings given then.)

Pupils are apt to take the Devil rather lightly, like some medieval elf or pixy. If so, ask if they take evil lightly. Why can't man make the progress he thinks he can? Why do people do the things they sometimes do? How can they be so cruel, outstripping any beast in their barbarity? Why can't we make some headway against selfishness and envy, pride and greed?

In the Bible Satan isn't always pictured as evil. Job 1 merely describes him as a tester. He seems more like a prosecuting attorney, an adversary, not necessarily bent on seducing. However, in the New Testament he is described as a deceiver and murderer, the "father of lies." You might ask pupils why he should resort to distortion and deception to accomplish his purposes—making the devilish appear godly and wrong appear right.

Note in the Lord's Prayer that the Seventh Petition probably refers to "the Evil One" when it says "Deliver us from evil." The word "evil" here is personified. We refer to the Devil as the source and embodiment of all evil.

3. Have pupils rephrase the petitions for their Prayer Notebooks.

In rephrasing the petitions studied today, center on the idea of "strength." Ask that prayers be focused on that theme and include in the notebooks. The collects under "Classic Prayers" in the Unit D introduction may be examined for emphases on "strength" and, if deemed suitable, included in the Prayer Notebooks.

4. Have a review period.

(a) Assist the class to sum up each petition in a single word—reverence, hope, submission, thanksgiving, forgiveness, strength; (b) indicate the various wordings of the Lord's Prayer; (c) restate the meaning of such terms as heaven, hallowed, kingdom of God, will of God, trespasses, temptations, evil; (d) rephrase various parts of the Lord's Prayer; (e) use questions such as:

Why do we use "trespasses" instead of "debts"?
How would you explain our use of the Doxology?
Why do we speak of God as "in heaven"?
Where is the kingdom of God?
Is everything that happens God's will?
If daily bread comes without praying, why do we pray for it?
What connection does God have with our temptation?

5. Conclude the Unit

In such time as may be left gather up loose ends. This may include checking on memory work (this could otherwise be incorporated into the review period). Since this term's memorization is limited to the Lord's Prayer, deadlines can be extended into the next two units.

You may also solicit pupil reaction to these studies. Do they feel that they know the Lord's Prayer better? Can they think of deeper implications when they use it? Do they feel greater ease in rephrasing it for their own sentence prayers?

6. Make assignments for the next session.

Ask pupils to read Chapter 25 and the Bible passages and to write out a list of all the reasons people give for going or not going to church.

UNIT OBJECTIVES

1. To help the pupil explore and understand the nature and purpose of public worship.

2. To assist him in deepening his appreciation and use of the various elements of worship.

3. To help him enrich his participation in public worship through a growing familiarity with such tools of worship as symbols, hymns, and the service book.

SCOPE OF UNIT

This unit links the study of prayer with the study of The Service in Unit G. Whereas the unit on prayer led into the Lord's Prayer, this unit on worship leads into the liturgy of the church. Two sessions (or three, if you have a 34-week school) are set for the unit.

The unit begins with general observations on public worship and moves into a study of two essential tools—symbols and the book used in public worship. In dealing with these tools, you will find more material than you can use. Once pupils show their expected interest in symbols, hymns, and rubrics, your problem will be to compress a vast body of material into your time limits.

Bear in mind that the first term dealt briefly with this field. Attention was given there to the church year, how a liturgy develops, and the meaning of altar and pulpit. Some review might be included in this unit, largely to bring the former study to life again.

STRUCTURE OF THE UNIT

If ample materials are at hand, this unit could be more pupil-led than previous units. A sufficient number of research projects is suggested below to allow considerable session time for pupil reports. You may even wish to allow time within the session for research studies, especially if you have only single copies of various resource books.

Session 25 has an introductory quiz and majors on constructing group worship. The additional session, which comes next, centers on the *Service Book and Hymnal*. Session 26 should find the group in the church sanctuary exploring visual symbols.

Bible study will offer biblical foundations for symbols and hymns. A "riddle-solving" approach (asking pupils to match Bible reference with symbol or hymn and seeing how closely they really do match) may be used. You have an opportunity here to excite pupils' interest in the frequent allusions to the Bible that may be found in hymn, prayer, symbol, and other materials of worship.

Pupils may work singly, in pairs, or threes on various projects and in constructing group worship. Dates for reports should be made at the outset.

MATERIALS NEEDED

Various books on symbols, hymns, and worship should be available for this unit. Your pastor may have copies in his library or your church may own or want to own certain standard works. The following would be most helpful:

Symbols and Terms of the Church, Edgar S. Brown, Jr. Inexpensive paperbound edition. Consider the possibility of getting a copy for each pupil.)

The Church at Worship, E. T. Horn, III

Worship, Luther D. Reed.

Christ and the Fine Arts, Cynthia Pearl Maus

Gospel in Hymns, Albert Edward Bailey

The Lutheran Liturgy, Luther D. Reed

Catalogues published by church publication houses illustrate figure symbols and so do occasional church bulletins.

The hymnal or service book used in the public worship of your congregation should be available, one to a pupil. While this unit assumes that the *Service Book and Hymnal* will be used, it would take only mild changes to apply every reference to your own book.

Bibles and concordances; chalkboard; ample supply of paper and pencils; Prayer Notebooks.

RESEARCH PROJECTS

More research projects are suggested that can possibly be used in the class sessions. Instead of assigning all eight, ask for volunteers for two or three projects, and refer to others as fascinating areas for independent research.

Spot Check of Worship.

This would involve keeping some record over several Sundays of who worships at church, and then compiling the results. Arrangements would have to be made with pastor and/or church officials for permission. If cards could be signed by worshipers over three or four Sundays, it would be the best way of getting a picture of a worshiping congregation. If that proves impossible, you might ask if pupils could have access to cards signed at the last communion service.

The project would involve an analysis of the cards. How many worshipers come from within one mile of the church, how many from between one and two miles, etc.? How many men and how many women? What per cent of members attend? How many teen-agers? How many don't attend at all? (A report like this might be of interest to others outside the class too.)

Symbols in Your Church.

This would involve a close examination of the church itself and of vestments and paraments. The chancel area and stained glass windows may be places for most symbols in the building. Pupils would not only list them, but attempt to learn their significance as Christian symbols.

Studies of Groups of Symbols.

Four or five separate studies may be undertaken here, depending on the resource material available. Areas for study include: (*a*) symbols of the four Evangelists; (*b*) types of crosses; (*c*) figure symbols; (*d*) symbols for the apostles; (*e*) Trinity symbols. Pupils should not only list the symbols, but indicate how they came to be used—why they stand for what they do. If pupils are artistic, they might even bring in drawings.

Floor Plan of the Church.

If done in the previous term, omit it here. Otherwise, ask pupils to identify various areas of the church together with chief furnishings. It need not be done to scale.

Stories Behind Hymns.

Here again the local resources will determine the extent of this project. If you have several books on hymns and hymn tunes at hand, you could ask two or three groups to work on this, making sure that their selections don't duplicate one another. Ask only that hymns selected be ones used in your church. For a starter you could suggest "O Love that wilt not let me go" (402) or "Just as I am, without one plea" (370).

Hymn Writers.

Several projects of this kind could be undertaken, with encyclopedia and books on hymns as the chief resources. You might suggest that pupils choose hymn writers with five or more hymns in the hymnal (such as Charles Wesley or Isaac Watts or Paul Gerhardt).

Tune Composers.

Follow the same procedure used in "Hymn Writers."

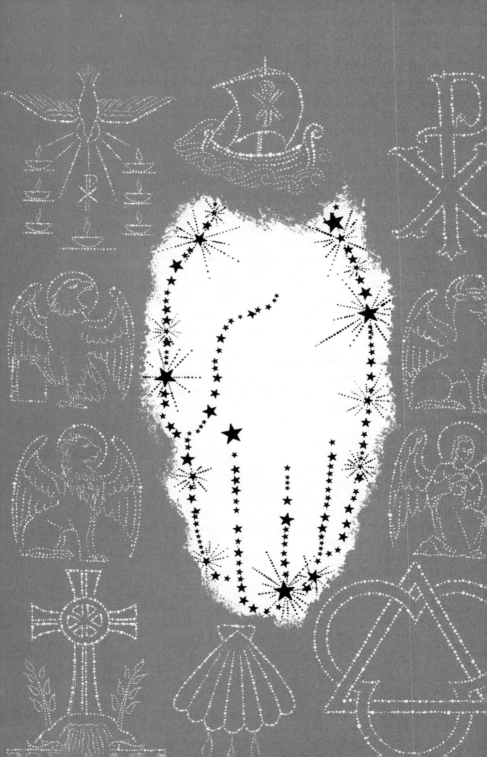

Variety of Hymns.

From church bulletins of the last year, pupils may list the number of different hymns used and their frequency. This study would indicate what per cent of the hymns in the hymnal is used. It may have interest for the whole congregation.

CONSTRUCTING GROUP WORSHIP

By this stage pupils should have had some experience in planning worship for the class session. However, this project is not designed for the pupils' period of worship, but to help them apply certain principles they study in this unit—such as harmony, dignity, progression (see Session 25).

Pupils could work in small groups to plan a short service around a common theme. A variety of themes and occasions could be suggested, such as: the key themes of parts of the Lord's Prayer; Jesus as the light of the world; an outdoors occasion; evening worship; concern for the needy; race relations; daily work.

A general discussion should precede their actual work. Ask how they would go about preparing a service for their local youth group. Suppose they were planning an outdoor theme? Which hymns would they choose? What would enter into their prayers? Where could they find further suggestions? What sort of Scripture lesson would they look for? What other materials would they include (such as responsive reading, Lord's Prayer)? How would they set a mood before the Scripture lesson? How would they set the spirit of worship?

After such a discussion you might ask them to break into groups and construct just such a service. They may need some assistance in finding suitable Scripture passages and responsive readings, but as long as they make a real effort to find something fitting, overlook the stumbling and fumbling. Attempt to get them to recognize such elements as the fitness of various materials, the sense of worship established, the pattern in fitting various parts together.

The theme may then be changed and another attempt made—this time with a theme from the Lord's Prayer, where Bible passages from the previous unit could aid them.

Several sessions could well be spent on this project. Extend it, if need be, into the next unit.

If you have resourceful pupils, you may suggest their thinking of ways to enrich the worship—what they would provide for visual attention, the use of symbols and art, both in flat pictures and by means of audio-visual aids. An example of such a service might be demonstrated as part of the group's own devotions in some future session.

Prayer Notebooks could be used for copying pupils' efforts at constructing such services. Include the pattern of worship, suggested hymns and Scripture readings, and prayers (sentence prayers or collects or both).

---

session 25

SCOPE OF SESSION

This session considers various elements of public worship, the purpose and importance of worship, and Bible teachings on worship. If you follow a thirty-session year, include some of the additional session in this period, reserving the balance for Session 26 and making such adjustments as may be needed. If you have a 34-session year, allow full period time for this and for the additional session which follows.

MATERIALS NEEDED

Resources suggested under the unit introduction should be arranged on tables, with as many such resources on hand as can be procured. While they may not be used in the session itself, pupils will need them for research projects.

Paper and pencils. Chalkboard. Bibles. Pupil's book (Chapter 25).

AN OVERVIEW OF THE SESSION

1. Test pupils on their knowledge of public worship.
2. Ask why pupils come to church and what they get out of it.
3. Study Bible passages to determine true worship.
4. Using the pupil's book, focus attention on some important elements of worship—chiefly, that worship is an act, that worthy worship requires harmony, dignity, and progression.
5. Ask pupils to construct worship for group devotions.
6. Outline research projects for the unit.
7. Make assignments for the next session.

SESSION PLAN IN GREATER DETAIL

1. Have a quiz.

If you wish, add questions of your own to the ones given below. Ask that papers be turned in without names. This will help you see on which points pupils are weak. Go over the answers quickly. If the quiz raises questions, answer them briefly, but ask that pupils hold them until pertinent material is studied.

a) What is the name for the part of the church where the altar stands? (The sanctuary, or chancel.)
b) Why do we follow certain Bible readings with the Gloria Patri? (To give a Christian ending to passages not essentially Christian [like the Psalms].)

148

c) *Why does the minister face one way for certain parts of worship, and another way for other parts?* (In one case he's speaking to God for the people, in the other he's speaking to the people for God.)

d) *What is a missal book?* (The altar service book on the "missal stand" on the altar.)

e) *What is (1) the narthex, (2) the nave, (3) a surplice, (4) a stole?* ([1] The vestibule of the church. [2] The seating area of the church. [3] The white robe worn by ministers over the black cassock. [4] The long ribbon in seasonal colors worn around the neck of the minister.)

f) *Of what are we reminded by (1) the cross, (2) candles, (3) a lamb carrying a banner, (4) a dove, (5) the letters IHS?* ([1] Christ's death for us. [2] Jesus as the light of the world. [3] Christ as the "Lamb of God." [4] The Holy Spirit. [5] the first three letters of the Greek name for Jesus.)

g) *What events or passages in the Bible do the following hymns remind you of?*

    (1) "While shepherds watched their flocks by night" (24)
    (2) "O God of Bethel" (or "O God of Jacob") (519)
    (3) "Lord, who at Cana's wedding feast" (301)
    (4) "O sacred Head, now wounded" (88)
    (5) "Come, ye faithful, raise the strain" (106)
    (6) "Brightest and best of the sons of the morning" (53)
    (7) "The King of love my shepherd is" (530)
    (8) "O God, our help in ages past" (168)
    (9) "As pants the hart for cooling streams" (388)
    (10) "O Jesus, thou art standing" (386)

([1] Christmas. [2] Genesis 28. [3] Changing water into wine, John 2. [4] The Crucifixion. [5] The Resurrection. [6] The wise men at Bethlehem. [7] Psalm 23. [8] Psalm 90. [9] Psalm 42. [10] Revelation 3:20.)

h) *What is (1) Matins, (2) Vespers?* ([1] The service appointed for early morning. [2] The service appointed for afternoon or evening.)

i) *What does the word "rubrics" mean?* (Instructions for worship —the name resembles "ruby" because rubrics were once printed in red.)

j) *What do we mean by "sacrificial" and "sacramental"?* (Sacrificial refers to our offering of prayer, praise, means, and self to God; sacramental refers to God's communication of himself to us.)

2. Ask pupils their reasons for churchgoing.

List reasons submitted by pupils on the chalkboard and then ask them to weigh various reasons. Which are worthy? Which less worthy? How often are people moved by one, how often by another? Pupils may cite sense of duty, force of habit, talking with God, making social contacts, family pressure, a special event like a baptism or anniversary, seeing old friends, feeling that the week would be incomplete without it.

Stress the voluntary nature of worship and good motivations for coming to church. Contrast poor motives, such as seeking entertainment values, looking for personal gain, coming to be seen by others. Which motives are strongest for your pupils? How often would they attend if there were no pressure of family or imminent confirmation? Attention may also be given worshipers' participation—whether good, bad, or indifferent in singing, praying, spirit of reverent attention to Bible and sermon. How would the congregation rate on such scores? What could be done to improve it? Pupils might also indicate what they like most and least in the worship of the church. Isn't this matter of like and dislike a clue to the way a person participates in worship?

Think of your own answers to these questions, sharing your feelings with the pupils, indicating how important worship is to you. Your own testimony will count far more than any lecture about its importance. Does it help you see things as they really are? Does it give you a vision of God himself? Does it get your values straightened out? Does it lift you up for the week?

3. Study Bible passages related to worship.

Three of the passages (Amos, Isaiah, and Matthew) seem to minimize worship in favor of right attitudes and deeds. Ask if these passages would rule out worship. Or do they insist strongly on the connection of worship with life? Amos pictures God as wanting no religious festivals so long as his people continued their evil practices. Isaiah makes worship appear as a life of social concern. Jesus wants deeds that tie in with words. In all three instances, worship is a sham unless it moves toward a changed life and attitude.

Jesus' own example in worship is set forth in the passages from Luke 19, John 7, and Luke 22. Note his observance of festivals and holy days. Note also his act to restore the Temple to its real function (after cleansing the Temple, he taught in it daily). These passages should serve to balance the three passages which may seem negative. Actually, they aren't negative. The emphasis is not so much on throwing out worship because it can be abused, but on keeping alive its true spirit. This Bible study will lead you to the central passage, John 4:19–24.

In connection with John 4, ask if it's wrong to associate public worship with special places. Is a church building any holier than other property? Why, or why not? Is it largely a matter of our association with special places? Is God more present in the church (like Mount Gerizim) than elsewhere? Some pupils may think this gives scriptural support to worshiping God out on a lakeside or picnic spot. Does it? Does such an idea really lead to worship there—or to forgetting God entirely? Does Jesus' reply indicate that God can't be worshiped on Mount Gerizim at all? Or that worship isn't restricted to that spot?

The importance of worshiping heart lies behind all this. No special place can guarantee true worship, even though it may help. It's the worship of the heart that really counts.

150

4. See the features of worship.

(If you are incorporating part of the additional session in this class period, omit this step.)

Only three features are mentioned in Chapter 25, largely for the construction of group devotions. You may want pupils to consider other features, especially those stemming from the Bible study. A spirit of reverence would be one, absence of distractions (or proper setting) another, and awareness of God's presence a third.

You might arrive at the same conclusion by asking what spoils worship for the pupils. They might point out things like the "botching" of music, the obtrusiveness of a worshiper, loud talking and laughter, dullness in reading or speaking.

The three features here may seem unclear to pupils until they begin constructing group devotions. Examples might be given of what happens when these features are ignored (as is done in Chapter 25), but don't expect pupils to appreciate them fully until they have tried their own hand.

5. Involve in constructing group worship.

This may be done as a class group or by dividing into smaller groups. Ask that pupils work on a common theme, following suggestions in the unit introduction.

6. Outline unit research projects.

Outline research projects for the unit, using the chalkboard for listing projects, describing each in some detail, assigning report dates, suggesting resources, and asking groups of pupils to undertake the projects. (See the unit introduction for this.)

If you cover the whole unit in two sessions, omit this step. However, you may list projects on a blackboard, suggesting that pupils make their own private investigation.

7. Make assignments for the next session.

If you are not using the additional session, assign the reading of Chapter 26 and the Bible references. Otherwise, ask the pupils to look through the *Service Book and Hymnal* to see the many different services and worship resources it contains.

---

an additional session for unit F (optional)
SCOPE OF SESSION

The study of The Service comes in the next unit so don't infringe on it here. At best, you can only give your pupils a brief introduction to the *Service Book and Hymnal*. You may not progress much farther than the whetting of appetites for deeper study of hymns, but this in itself will be a considerable achievement, since a lifelong interest may get its start right here. This session will, therefore, be one of sampling— a taste of hymns, hymn tunes, hymn writers, services for various occasions, instructions for worship.

MATERIALS NEEDED

Resources suggested under the unit introduction. Copies of the *Service Book and Hymnal*. Bibles. Prayer Notebooks. Pupil's book (Chapter 26).

AN OVERVIEW OF THE SESSION

1. *Use Chapter 26 to talk about hymns and hymn tunes.*
2. *Have pupils examine the index of writers and composers.*
3. *Match Bible passages with hymn titles.*
4. *Let pupils become more familiar with Matins, Vespers, and Suffrages.*
5. *Have the pupils read in the General Rubrics (pp. 274–284) at the end of the service book quietly, looking for places where the local church may vary.*
6. *Conclude with further construction of group worship, adding findings to Prayer Notebooks.*
7. *Make assignments for the next session.*

SESSION PLAN IN GREATER DETAIL

1. *Use Chapter 26 to talk about hymns and hymn tunes.*

The mechanics of matching tunes and words will interest pupils. As a sample of various meters, you might cite "O God our help in ages past" (168) for Common Meter; "I love thy kingdom, Lord" (158) for Short Meter; and the familiar Doxology "Praise God from whom all blessings flow" (602) for Long Meter. When pupils try these words with other tunes of the same meter, they will see the purpose for this notation in hymnals. Let them match the words of "It came upon the midnight clear" (23) with "While shepherds watched their flocks by night" (24) as a sample. If any pupils have sung in school choruses, they will know the tune "Greensleeves," which is the tune for "What child is this" (48) in the *Service Book and Hymnal*. This would be further example of the importance of notations on hymns.

2. *Have pupils look at the index of writers and composers.*

As pupils look at the index of writers and composers, indicate the wide variety in nationality, church affiliation, and century of these people. Ask if such knowledge makes any real difference in pupils' feeling for a hymn. Like many passages of the Bible, the content is the central value—not who did the writing or when or where. While such information helps in our appreciation, it isn't necessary to our use of hymns. If there is any place where distinctions of creed and national backgrounds are overridden, it is within the covers of a hymnal. Such a discussion should add to the pupils' feeling for the hymnal as an aid to worship.

3. *Have pupils match Bible passages with hymn titles.*

List the Bible passages given below on a chalkboard. Ask pupils to look them up and match them with hymn titles. Ask if pupils can locate other hymns with biblical basis (Psalm number under hymn indicates this Bible basis in the *Service Book and Hymnal*).

All passages match hymn titles, except for Exodus 40:34–38, which is the basis for an allusion in "Glorious things of thee are spoken." The seven passages, with hymns and hymn numbers in the *Service Book and Hymnal* are:

> *Revelation 4:8–11 "Holy, holy, holy" (131)*
> *Revelation 7:9–12 "Blessing and honor" (166)*
> *Psalm 90 "Our God, our help in ages past" (168)*
> *Psalm 42 "As pants the hart for cooling streams" (388)*
> *Genesis 28:10–22 "O God of Bethel" (519)*
> *Isaiah 41:8–10 "How firm a foundation" (558)*
> *Exodus 40:34–38 "Glorious things of thee are spoken" (152), third stanza.*

Hymns should be studied as paraphrases of the passages—attempts to put the passages in rhymed form. See the list "Psalm Paraphrases" on page 284 of the *Service Book and Hymnal.*

4. Study other orders of worship.

Pupils should grow more and more familiar with general contents of the service book. By now they should be familiar with the location of The Service, with the Propers for the church year, with Psalms and Collects. Three orders are suggested here, since pupils may begin to use them—speaking them if not singing them—in group worship. Have them note the general flavor of Matins and Vespers, each reflecting a time of day, also the fitness of Morning and Evening Suffrages. If your church uses any of these orders, ask if pupils have participated. (Lenten services often use Vespers, as do youth services in the evening.)

5. Examine the General Rubrics.

Instructions given in italics before the Order for Marriage might provide a sample of the use of rubrics. Have pupils note these instructions.

As they read over the General Rubrics, you may point out interesting angles, bearing in mind the distinction between "shall" and "may."

7. Make assignments for the next session.

Assign the reading of Chapter 26 and the Bible references. Ask pupils to be prepared to talk about what they like best in The Service and what their impressions are of worship in their church.

---

session 26
SCOPE OF SESSION

Symbols—their identification and meaning and use as a tool of worship—provide the focus of this session. Part of the period should be spent in the church sanctuary, considering symbols of your local church and, if possible, having the pastor serve as a resource person. Pupils' reports on research projects will guide the session.

MATERIALS NEEDED

Whatever resources on church symbolism you find available. If a brochure of your own church describes symbols in the building, it would be invaluable. Church bulletins often make considerable use of these worship aids.

Bibles. Prayer Notebooks. Pupil's book (Chapter 26).

AN OVERVIEW OF THE SESSION

1. *Use the church sanctuary for an investigation of symbols in your local church.*
2. *Discuss sections of Chapter 26.*
3. *Match Bible passages with symbols suggested for each.*
4. *Have pupils list symbols from your own church in their Prayer Notebooks.*
5. *Devote further time to completing work on group devotions.*
6. *Make assignments for the next session.*

SESSION PLAN IN GREATER DETAIL

1. Investigate symbols in your own church.

The number and kinds of symbols should be surprising to pupils. Arrange to have some of the altar hangings (or some illustrations of their designs) available for display purposes. Don't overlook such seemingly inconsequential items as the number of steps to the altar, the cross and orb on the front of the *Service Book and Hymnal,* the number of sides for a baptismal font, the panels in or behind the altar. Chapter 26 will help you explain many of these symbols. If the pastor is available, ask that he explain any symbols the group doesn't understand.

Identification of church furnishings may be for review purposes if pupils studied this last term. Pupils should be able to identify chancel, narthex, nave, altar, pulpit, retable, lectern, font, communion rail, and perhaps a few of the items used during the celebration of the Lord's Supper such as chalice, nost, ciborium.

2. Discuss the sections of Chapter 26.

On returning to class area, discuss Chapter 26 of the pupil's book, with its emphasis on "code language" and "in the know." Are the meanings of symbols really clear? Should they be? How many are readily understood by the average church member? If pupils have prepared reports on other symbols and their meaning, such reports might be given now.

While many symbols suggested here have already been discussed in the church sanctuary, you might ask if pupils see any different meaning now. Are the symbols really clear, or does it take a detective to find their real meaning? Should we use symbols that convey a different meaning from the one intended? (A case in point is the three rings borrowed by a beer advertisement from church sources.) Allow room for difference of opinion on such issues. However, help pupils feel that "code language" (symbols) is intended for those who understand the code, and is valuable even though outsiders may not understand it.

You might also ask if a church can have too many symbols, or too many strange symbols. When symbols begin to call attention to themselves and not to what is symbolized, they lose their place. Instead of aiding worship, they then distract. A dozen crosses may appear unobtrusively in a church, but if there were a hundred, it might make you think of a military cemetery.

3. Match Bible passages with symbols.

Here's a place to indicate how many church symbols are derived from biblical associations. The church borrows heavily from tradition, especially in shields of the apostles and saints, but it's usually tradition that is in harmony with Scripture.

Greek letters may puzzle pupils unless they have been exposed to fraternity names. Have the pupils draw the *alpha* and *omega*, the *XP* and the *IHS* in their notebooks. You might indicate how the Greek alphabet begins with *alpha* and ends with *omega* (the Gloria Patri alludes to this symbol of beginning and ending). In the *XP* note that the *X* is a Greek letter, *Chi*, which is equivalent to "Ch" in English; the *P* is the Greek *rho*, which is the same as our "r." Thus "Chr" is the first part of the name of Christ.

The winged creatures of Revelation (also of Ezekiel) are the symbols for the four Evangelists, though they are not always the same. The Gospel of John is the winged eagle because it soars to great heights; the winged man suggests the humanity of Christ, depicted in Matthew. The winged lion is for St. Mark, descriptive of the royal character of Christ; the winged ox or calf represents St. Luke in his account of our Lord's sacrifice. One can see how these figures can be interchanged, but the four have long been linked with the Gospel writers. The tongues of fire in Acts 2:1-4 are symbolic of the Holy Spirit.

If a concordance is at hand, other symbols in your local church can be matched with supporting Bible verses (like candles with Jesus as the light of the world in John 12:46).

4. Let pupils add symbols to their Prayer Notebooks.

If there is time and the pupils are interested, have them list the symbols that they see in your church. As they write this list in their Prayer Notebooks, perhaps you would like to add a brief explanation of each. If pupils want to draw them, so much the better.

5. Continue work on constructing group devotions.

Devote further time to helping the pupils construct group devotions, completing the work they have done in the previous sessions.

6. Make assignments for the next session.

Ask pupils to read Chapter 27 and the Bible passages. Also give them these two questions to mull over during the week: (*a*) Which parts of The Service appeal to you most, and why? (*b*) What is your general impression of worship in your church?

UNIT OBJECTIVES

1. To help the pupil deepen his appreciation of the public worship of the church.

2. To help him understand in some detail the structure, elements, and drama of The Service.

3. To help him participate intelligently in public worship.

SCOPE OF UNIT

Three assumptions lie behind this unit: (1) that pupils already have a degree of familiarity with The Service through their study in Unit A and participation in church worship; (2) that they are reasonably familiar with the pattern and purpose of the church year, also with the process by which a liturgy comes into being (from Session 4); and (3) that The Service in one form or another is in common usage in your church—either in the *Service Book and Hymnal,* or in an earlier form such as the *Common Service Book.*

In the over-all pattern of this course, note the progression from a general study of prayer to the Lord's Prayer, then from a study of public worship to a study of the chief service of the church.

The four sessions of Unit G are devoted exclusively to The Service, first through a bird's-eye view of its pattern, then through a more detailed study of its various parts. The section on the Office of the Word will doubtless require more time than other parts, because of its length and its more frequent use by pupils. An additional session is provided for review of the course if your course goes beyond thirty sessions.

STRUCTURE OF THE UNIT

The four sessions are unequal. While the three traditional divisions of The Service are observed more attention could be given to the Office of the Word and Communion than to the Confession. One could easily divide the Office of the Word into Praise, Declaring the Word, and Offering and devote a session to each.

Keep the Service itself before the pupils at all times. This is their basic tool. If you feel that they need review of locating proper pages in the service book, some attention should be given to this. Attention should also be given, if needed, to review of the church year. Your aim is to provide as much familiarity with The Service in a four-session unit as you can, and at the same time open up areas for further study in later years. In terms of specific objectives, you will help the pupil develop:

An over-all picture of the pattern of The Service.

A feeling that something actually happens when we worship.

A sense of two peaks in worship—the proclamation of the Word and Holy Communion.

A feeling for the dignity of worship, together with its "objective" character (where God confronts us, rather than where we confront God).

At least a nodding acquaintance with terms common in public worship.

These objectives should help you structure your approach and teaching. You will need to define worship terms which can be added to the Prayer Notebook. Bible study should parallel parts of The Service. From time to time the over-all pattern should be reviewed to show how pupils have progressed in their study and to note the movement in The Service.

MATERIALS NEEDED

Books suggested for the previous unit apply to this unit also, especially:

The Lutheran Liturgy, Luther D. Reed

Living the Liturgy, Edgar S. Brown, Jr.

In your own preparation these books are invaluable—also as a reference authority for questions that may arise. If they do no more than give you a comfortable feeling in guiding the sessions, that should prove enough.

Each pupil should have a copy of the service book used in the public worship of your church. Bibles and Prayer Notebooks will be used.

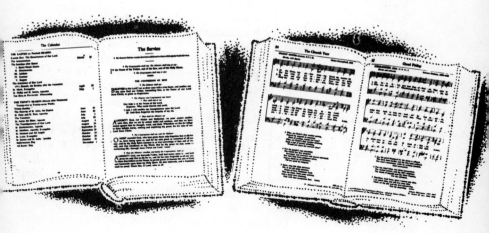

DISCUSSION STARTERS

In lieu of assigning research projects, have pupils give advance thought to discussion topics or questions that will be pertinent in various sessions. (Two such "discussion starters" were included in the homework assignment given at the end of Session 26, and will be drawn on in Session 27.) While you may want all pupils to give some thought to all questions, you may alternatively ask certain pupils to concentrate on specific questions—jotting down their thoughts, asking others how they would answer, and contributing their observations and thoughtful conclusions to the class discussion. At least one "discussion starter" is included in each homework assignment throughout the unit.

The questions themselves are open-ended, with no set conclusions implied and no assigned points of view to be defended.

GLOSSARY

A glossary of terms special to public worship may be necessary in this unit. Pupils could either include these terms and definitions in their Prayer Notebooks or make series of "flash cards," 3- by 5-inch cards with the term on one side and the definition on the reverse. Individual pupils could use the flash cards to check their understanding of the terms, and the whole class could use them for a spot review.

Most of the terms given below occur in the course of the unit. Pupils may add others that puzzle them. (Most dictionaries will carry adequate definitions, but it would be helpful to have the books listed under "Materials Needed" available.)

Gloria Patri	Gloria in Excelsis	Sanctus
Agnus Dei	Nunc Dimittis	Pax
Kyrie	Epistle	Gradual
Gospel	Introit	Collect
Offertory	Benediction	Versicles
Propers (or Pericopes)	Invocation	Verba (Words of
Chalice	Ciborium	Institution)
Paten	Flagon	Host
Ewer	Stole	Surplice
Cotta	Cassock	Parament
Sacramental	Sacrificial	

Also be alert for ordinary words that pupils may not yet know. The confessional services, for example, include: *ample, beseech, transgressions, iniquity, refuge, remission, grace, bestoweth, imploring, grievously, infirmities, amendment, repent.* These words are probably not in your seventh-graders' vocabularies; it is up to you to explain them. (Precise definitions are not needed, but the sense of a word should be made clear.) Encourage pupils to ask whenever they encounter a word whose meaning they do not know.

BIBLE STUDY

Portions of The Service that quote the Bible directly have already been included in Bible study (Session 4). They are not included again here, though you may profit by reviewing them.

If you wish to include other Bible passages used in this unit, the following might be added to the matching quiz in Session 27.

(1) Isaiah 6:2–3   Verba or Words of Institution (5)
(2) Matthew 9:27   Kyrie (2)
(3) 2 Corinthians 13:14   Sanctus (1)
(4) John 20:19–21   New Testament Benediction (3)
(5) 1 Corinthians 11:23–26   Pax (4)

Passages selected for sessions of this unit are illustrative of various parts of The Service. For example, Session 28 deals with confession and pardon, citing Bible passages of this character; while biblical examples of preaching, Scripture reading and the Kyrie find a place in Session 29.

The study of passages harmonized for the Words of Institution would make an interesting project in connection with Communion. Pupils might piece together Matthew 26:26–29, Mark 14:22–25, Luke 22:17–20, and 1 Corinthians 11:23–26 to see how these passages are meshed in The Service.

FOR INTERESTED PUPILS

Research projects are not vital for these sessions. However, you may want to offer interested pupils some topics they could profitably pursue. The following are, therefore, suggested. Do not press pupils to volunteer. Time for hearing any reports that may be prepared is allowed in Session 29.

1. The Bible in The Service. The pupils could develop a check list of biblical passages embodied in the liturgy. They could then move beyond into passages appointed for Introit, Gradual, and Scripture lessons. A concordance would be essential here, together with resource books on The Service.

2. The Epistles of the Church Year. Pupils would assemble information on the Epistles, including the listing of New Testament Epistles most frequently used and those not used at all.

3. The Gospels of the Church Year. Information similar to that gathered for the Epistles would be sought here. Some pupils might even want to see what important passages are omitted in the church year.

4. The Worship of Various Churches. Pupils who have close friends in other churches may find this appealing. One might make comparisons with an English translation of the Roman Catholic Mass; another, a comparison with less formal services used in other Protestant churches.

CONSTRUCTING GROUP WORSHIP

The exercise in constructing services for group worship could be continued throughout this unit. Such services could be used in the class's weekly worship. By this time, pupils should be adept enough to require little assistance—perhaps no more than occasional polishing.

---

session 27
SCOPE OF SESSION

Seeing The Service as a whole—its broad pattern, its progression, its high peaks—is the central concern here. This session should present a panoramic view, and succeeding sessions focus on details.

MATERIALS NEEDED

Copies of the *Service Book and Hymnal.* Bibles. Chalkboard. Prayer Notebooks. Pupil's book (Chapter 27).

AN OVERVIEW OF THE SESSION

1. Consider the discussion questions.
2. Examine the headings in The Service, pointing out major and minor divisions.
3. See the reasons behind the arrangement of The Service. Include a study of Isaiah 6.
4. Define puzzling worship terms and insert a glossary section in Prayer Notebooks.
5. Examine Bible passages for their emphasis on praise and adoration in worship.
6. Make assignments for the next session.

SESSION PLAN IN GREATER DETAIL

1. Discuss the questions given as homework.

Ask pupils to share what they like best about The Service. Which parts appeal to them? Why? What is their impression of worship in their church? Is it a joyful occasion? Solemn? Rather boring? Do worshipers participate fully, or do they seem like spectators? Do they seem to know what's going on? Encourage them to speak freely, with stronger emphasis on what they like than on what they dislike.

2. Outline The Service.

You might put the general outline of The Service on the chalkboard, having pupils note special headings in their service books. They should list:

Confession of Sins	Gospel
Introit	Creed
Gloria Patri	Hymn
Kyrie	Sermon
Gloria in Excelsis	Offering
Collect	Offertory
Epistle	Prayer of the Church
Gradual	Benediction

List also the headings in large and small type for the Communion Service.

Help pupils group these headings under the three parts: Confession, Office of the Word, Office of Communion. Ask for further division by questioning as to which are strictly Bible readings, which might be included under offerings, and which are primarily where God speaks and which where we respond.

As these parts are listed, ask why they are so named. This will provide you with a list of terms needed for the glossary. If pupils are puzzled, continue with the over-all structure before taking time to define terms.

3. Probe reasons for the structure of The Service.

In Session 4 pupils were asked how they would go about designing a service to meet the needs of worshipers. The section "Jigsaw" in Chapter 27 emphasizes this point. If the plan for worship were pupils' responsibility, what would they include and how would they arrange it? Would the pupils be satisfied with the four steps suggested in Chapter 27 and the way they're arranged?

Isaiah 6 provides a further analysis of a pattern in worship. You might put the following items on the chalkboard and ask which verses in Isaiah 6:1–8 correspond to them.

Being confronted by God (verses 1–4)
Sense of unworthiness (verse 5)
Assurance of pardon (verse 7)
Listening to God (verse 8)
Offering self in service (verse 8)

Ask pupils to interchange parts of this pattern and see how awkward it becomes.

When you feel that pupils have grasped the need for such a pattern and the orderliness behind it, refer them again to the parts of The Service. Failing to see the wood because of the trees, they may have felt little rhyme or reason behind the parts listed.

They may now be asked to identify the *sacramental* and *sacrificial* elements in The Service. The sacramental parts of The Service are where God speaks and we listen (indicated by the minister in facing the congregation); the sacrificial parts are where we speak and offer to God (where the minister faces the altar). God speaks through Word and Sacraments—therefore, these are sacramental. We speak through prayer, praise, and offering—sacrificial.

4. Have pupils enter glossary terms in their Prayer Notebooks.

In this session you may limit the glossary to terms used in the various headings. Most of them are Latin names for the opening words. *Kyrie,* the Greek word for "Lord," is the one exception. It is one place where the influence of the Eastern Church is present in The Service. In most cases no dictionary will be needed. Pupils may have to look up "Introit" and "Collect" and "Epistle" in a dictionary, but one pupil could do this for the entire group. Be sure you do this before you assign pupils to the task.

5. Examine Bible passages.

Before dealing with the passages you may want to use a matching quiz, numbering and lettering items in the two columns, and letting pupils correct their own papers. They should use their Bibles for this exercise, though it would be sporting to ask them *not* to use their service books. Their memory of glossary terms will be revealed in their answers.

The Major Chants of The Service

(1) Numbers 6:24–26	Gloria in Excelsis (4)
(2) Psalm 51:10–12	Agnus Dei (6)
(3) Psalm 32:5	Versicle in Confession (3)
(4) Luke 2:14	Benediction (1)
(5) Luke 2:29–31	Nunc Dimittis (5)
(6) John 1:29	Offertory (2)

Bible passages (except for Isaiah 6:1–8) emphasize various aspects of public worship, and also provide examples of worship in Bible times. Pupils might take some comfort in conditions cited in 1 Corinthians— the people of Corinth had their troubles too! But the main note of joy should be underscored—joy in the presence of God who deigns to commune with us in worship.

6. Make assignments for the next session.

Have the pupils read Chapter 28, study the Bible passages and be prepared to discuss their personal opinions about confession of sins. Does public confession take the place of private confession? Should the church insist on public confession? Private confession? Both? None?

162

session 28

SCOPE OF SESSION

The confessional part of the Service (up to the Introit) will be studied in detail during this session. It may not require the full session. Pace yourself so that you introduce parts of Session 29 within this period. Pupils should become more familiar with the three confessional services. One (SBH, pp. 1-2) is used when Communion is omitted, the other two (SBH, pp. 247-252) prior to communing.

MATERIALS NEEDED

Service books. Resource books suggested in the unit introduction. An English dictionary. Bibles. Pupil's book (Chapter 28).

AN OVERVIEW OF THE SESSION

1. Have pupils express their opinions on public and private confession. Ask them to read the section on Confession in the Small Catechism.

2. Have the pupils read the confessional part of The Service.

3. Use Chapter 28 to examine an explanation of various points in the Confession.

4. Discuss the alternate confessional services, noting in what ways they differ from services used when there is no Communion.

5. Explore the Bible passages.

6. Make assignments for the next session.

SESSION PLAN IN GREATER DETAIL

1. Have the pupils express their opinions about confession.

Ask the pupils for their feelings about confession. What values are in public confession? Help pupils feel that: (*a*) in public confession each person is identified with the common sins and sinfulness of the group; (*b*) each person, however, should personalize his confession to God, either in the privacy of his heart or openly to a Christian friend.

Lead to a discussion of the practice of private confession. Luther commended the practice. Have the pupils read what he has to say in the *Small Catechism*. Pupils may feel a certain aversion to confession because of its association with compulsion and prying. It it were voluntary, would they think more of it? Is it any the less "private confession" when people bare their souls to a pastor or fellow Christian without labeling it "confession"? You might indicate how the role of pastor often involves private confession, and how many laws respect the confidential nature of such a confession.

2. Have the pupils read the confessional part of The Service.

Pupils may be asked to rephrase parts here, using more familiar words where difficult ones are encountered. (One or two pupils may be assigned to look up difficult words and report to class while reading continues.) Maybe the group would like to translate the whole confessional part of The Service into their own vernacular.

Certain things may be noted here:

a) The invitation or exhortation to confession ("Beloved in the Lord, etc.") How else could it be said? "Dear Friends"? Why should the name of Jesus be brought in? Is "beseech" a stronger word than "ask"?

b) The two Versicles and Responses that set the stage for the confession. The second versicle might make more sense if "when" preceded it: *"When* I said, I will confess. . . ." It provides an assurance of God's pardon for sincere confession.

c) The priestly role of the minister in two paragraphs: in one, he faces the altar confessing the sin of the whole congregation to God; in the other, he faces the congregation declaring God's pardon to all who repent. Note the position of the minister in each instance. (Note his post at the bottom of the chancel steps, if your church observes this practice.)

d) The general nature of the confession. In effect, it says that we are powerless to help ourselves, and that our sins include every area—"thought, word, and deed." Except for God's mercy we have no right to approach him, no claims on his pardon.

e) The group nature of the congregation's confession. Whereas in the confession before communing each person says "I," here each person says "we," Note what is asked—not only pardon, but the gift of the Holy Spirit and conformity to his leadership.

f) The power of the "declaration of grace." God not only forgives us, but imparts power. He takes us fully into his good graces, and gives us his Holy Spirit.

3. Review the explanation of the Confession in Chapter 28 of the pupil's book.

Your use of this chapter will depend on whether pupils have read the chapter prior to the session. It helps explain what lies behind the Confession, as well as the separate parts of this service. Pupils might be asked whether this part of The Service seems clearer through such an explanation. Underscore the idea of our unworthiness to come before God—an idea further considered in the Bible passages.

4. Discuss the alternate confessional services.

Have the pupils look at the alternate confessional services in the *Service Book and Hymnal,* (pp. 247-252). Note that the longer Order or Public Confession is designed to be used as a full service in itself. (Some churches have confessional services a day or two prior to Communion, especially during Holy Week.)

Note, too, the more personal character of confession here since it precedes the more personal gift of the Word in the sacrament.

Observe also its inclusion of "secret thoughts and desires" (as in Psalm 139) which our very sinfulness prevents us from seeing. Sins of

164

impulse come in here too, where we don't know why we do what we do. (Pupils can give some examples of this—the spur of the moment impulse that overtakes them.)

It may be pointed out that this confession is usually in kneeling position. The very posture adds extra meaning to the confession.

The "declaration of grace" here includes more direct references to the pardoning act of Christ as authority for coming before God and receiving his gift.

Note too that these "alternate" confessional services close with a benediction, indicating that they are complete services, separate from what may follow.

5. Explore Bible passages.

Psalm 24 may be studied as a liturgical song sung as the congregation approached the temple. Have pupils imagine the temple doors closed, with passwords needed to have them opened (as in verses 7-10). Note also the requirements for coming into the temple (verse 4). Do we need passwords in Christian worship?

Other passages from the Psalms voice ancient confessions and requirements for approaching God. Would pupils recognize Psalm 51 in the confession of the prodigal? (See Luke 15:11 ff. if they are hazy on this.) Psalm 139:23-24 may be saved for the confession prior to communing.

Ask if pupils see any resemblance between Hebrews 10:19-25 and the language of the preparatory service (e.g., drawing near with a true heart—the use of biblical phrasing in seemingly incidental parts of the liturgy).

Romans 10:9-13 might be examined to see if confession with the lips is really enough. Is this all that Paul meant?

6. Make assignments for the next session.

Ask pupils to read Chapter 29 and the Bible passages carefully. Ask them to think about one of the following questions: (a) Should the church use modern translation of the Bible in The Service? What would be gained and what lost? Does it really make any difference? Which translation is used in your church? (b) What do you expect in a sermon?

---

session 29
SCOPE OF THE SESSION

For most pupils The Service means the liturgy without Communion, since the sacrament is administered no more than a dozen times a year in most churches. Strictly speaking, therefore, they know The Service in its brief form—with the Benediction following immediately after the Prayer of the Church and the Lord's Prayer.

This session considers the Office of the Word, beginning with the Introit and concluding with the Prayer of the Church. It's a rather extensive area to cover and could well spill over into other sessions. Moreover, you may wish to treat it in four divisions, as indicated below.

MATERIALS NEEDED

Service books. Bibles. Prayer Notebooks. Chalkboard. Dictionaries. Resource books and lectionaries if special assignments by interested pupils are to be reported (see the unit introduction). Pupil's book (Chapter 29).

AN OVERVIEW OF THE SESSION

1. Review the over-all picture of The Service.
2. Lead the pupils in a detailed study of the Office of the Word. Discuss Bible translations and the function of the sermon.
3. Provide opportunities for pupils to make reports on special assignments.
4. Make assignments for the next session.

SESSION PLAN IN GREATER DETAIL

1. Review the over-all picture of The Service.

Use a chalkboard if possible (or the outline in pupil's book, Chapter 27) and note divisions of the Office of the Word for study in this session.

2. Lead the pupils in studying the Office of the Word

Help the pupils see the four main divisions of this office.
a) Introit through Collect.

This division merits extensive treatment, since it involves terms like Introit, Gloria Patri, Gloria in Excelsis, Kyrie, Collect. Make sure pupils are able to identify each. The pupil's book should help them understand the purpose and place for each, e.g., why we follow Old Testament passages with the Gloria Patri; what the dominant tone of the Gloria in Excelsis is; why the Kyrie comes between the two Glorias; why a collect is so named. The Bible passage from Matthew 9 illustrates the Kyrie. You may also allude to Isaiah 6, indicating how God confronted Isaiah in the Temple and how, in much the same way, God confronts us through the Introit. Therefore, the Introit marks the beginning of The Service itself.

b) Lessons through the Creed.

Ask if pupils can find any Epistle lesson *not* from a New Testament epistle (that for Pentecost from the Book of Acts is one of the few instances). Let a pupil look up "epistle," asking why we don't call letters epistles today. An epistle is a formal letter written in elegant style, usually for teaching purposes. Few personal letters would ever fall into this category.

Certain practices might be discussed there: the congregation's standing for the Gospel and sitting for the Epistle (to give the reading of the Gospel greater status, since it comes from the words and deeds of our Lord): the brief responses that surround the reading of the Gospel; the purpose of a Gradual between these two lessons (to provide a step from lower to higher).

Ask the pupils for their opinions about using modern translations of the Bible in The Service. If you have several modern Bible translations you might have both Epistle and Gospel for the coming Sunday read from these translations, drawing comparisons with the version used in your own church. This would give pupils a specific basis for indicating their tastes and reasons for their choice.

If pupils have investigated the coverage of Epistles and Gospels (see unit introduction, "For Interested Pupils"), they could report on passages covered. Except for passages in the book of Acts, the New Testament is adequately covered through these appointed lessons; the practice of reading an Old Testament lesson has closed a gap for that section of the Bible. This protects a congregation from a narrow, somewhat biased choice that might result if it were left up to the pastor alone. Moreover, it centers attention squarely where it belongs—in the life, teachings, and work of our Lord.

c). The Hymn through the Sermon.

Note that this is the only place in The Service where a hymn is referred to as The Hymn. It is chosen for its link with the sermon—sometimes to anticipate the punch line, sometimes to provide a mood. Pupils might be interested in the suggestions for hymns for each Sunday listed in the back of the service book (SBH, p. 1004). Here are suggestions that provide a basis of choice for the hymns sung today. (You might have the class look up the suggested hymns for the coming Sunday to see how many are actually chosen. And if time permits, discuss the method of selecting hymns used in your church.)

Ask the pupils for their opinions on the purpose and place. Ask what they look for in the sermon. Do they regard it as good if it entertains and is interesting? If it hits home with some truth? If it explains the Bible? If it leaves them with a feeling of wanting to do something about it?

Bible passages from Romans and Acts might be studied here. Are Paul's comments about preaching as meaningful today as when he wrote to the church at Rome? The two sermons in Acts show examples of the preaching of Peter and Paul.

d) Offering through the Prayer of the Church.

Ask pupils how many different things they can offer the Lord as a way of saying "thank you" for his gifts. Let them put their suggestions on the chalkboard. You will probably get answers like money, food, clothing, property. Guide the class to see that prayer and praise are offerings to God, as is the dedication of the whole life. The money that we put in the offering plate is symbolic of this self-giving.

167

The Offertory from Psalm 51 ("Create in me") emphasizes the personal involvement in any offering to God. In The Service the offertory is part and parcel of the offering. In earlier days when offerings included gifts of food, wine, clothing, as well as money, the offertory served a unique purpose. After gifts were brought to the altar, and while the congregation sang Psalm 51, the priest would take bread and wine from among the gifts to prepare them for the Communion. In our present use, the offertory conveys the idea of our money gifts as a token of our self-offering.

Give the Prayer of the Church fairly close examination. Though the printed prayer may be used only on Communion and Festival Sundays in your church, it is still a model for all such general prayers. Have pupils note its pattern: adoration and thanksgiving; a series of intercessions for the church, the state and its leaders, the needy; and finally petitions for ourselves. Compare its pattern with that of the Lord's Prayer, especially on the low priority given to personal petitions. Suggest this as a pattern for private prayer.

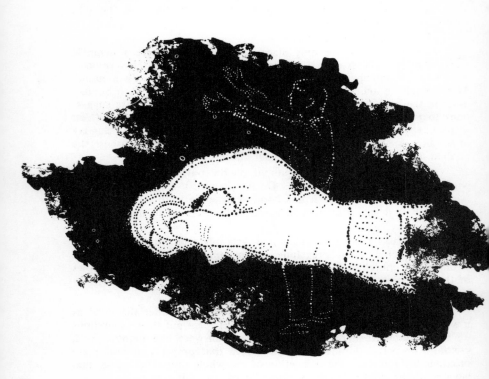

3. Provide opportunities for reports.

If pupils have volunteered for special assignments (see the unit introduction, "For Interested Pupils"), they may bring in their findings here. Be sure to allow enough time for this.

4. Make assignments for the next session.

Ask pupils to read Chapter 30 and the Bible passages and to think about this question: What qualifies a person for Communion?

---

session 30
SCOPE OF THE SESSION

Pupils have not yet studied the sacraments in detail. You, therefore, will not want to probe too deeply into what will be studied later. Your immediate aim is to help the pupils deepen their understanding and appreciation of the liturgical portions of The Communion, beginning with the Preface and concluding with the Benediction. This will involve not only becoming familiar with chants and responses, but also becoming aware that what God does in the sacrament is more important than what man does.

Read carefully Chapter 30 of the pupil's book. It can be used as a session guide.

AN OVERVIEW OF THE SESSION

1. Ask pupils for their reactions to the Communion.
2. Discuss the importance of Communion to Lutherans.
3. Examine the Communion liturgy in The Service, noting glossary terms in the Prayer Notebooks, and the over-all structure.
4. Explore the Bible passages.
5. Discuss questions related to participating in Communion.
6. If this is the final session, use material from the additional session in this unit to provide a review of the course.

SESSION PLAN IN GREATER DETAIL

1. Ask for reactions to the Communion.

Using "Reactions, Please" in the pupil's book as a springboard, ask if pupils have attended Communion Services, what their reactions are, what they expect in Communion.

Impression with the solemnity and mystery of the sacrament are two common reactions, both very much in place. Perhaps you can draw pupils' attention to "The Thanksgiving" as the heading for the Communion liturgy—indicating the joy in it. Communion hymns might be examined for this note of joy (also note the parables of Jesus that refer to a heavenly banquet or great supper). You may also suggest that various seasons sharpen certain aspects of communing (Lent has a solemn tone, even as the Last Supper; but Easter is joyful; World-Wide Communion suggests the social aspects of Christians united around the world in the sacrament).

If pupils expect something magical to happen, indicate what communing means to you; also that, while bread remains bread and wine remains wine, Christ comes to us in a very real way. Moreover, his presence is given to us through the entire Communion, not just at the moment when the minister speaks the Words of Institution or when the worshiper eats the bread and drinks the wine.

Through these reactions of pupils you will be guided in dealing with the Communion liturgy — where to correct wrong impressions, where to lay special emphasis, etc.

2. Discuss the importance of Communion.

The first two sections of the pupil's book set the tone for this. You may go beyond them to such indications as the practice of private Communion among Lutherans, the importance given to communing membership (as a barometer of spiritual health), the increased attendance at Communion Services.

The whole life and faith of a church come to sharp focus in the Lord's Supper. This is why the sacrament has so often been a battlefield among churches. What we believe about God, his Word, the cross, the church—all has a bearing here, for worship reflects doctrine and is expressive of the faith of the church. You may, therefore, feel that the whole compass of the Christian faith could come within your scope; and you can't entirely avoid that.

Ours is a sacramental church. The thrust of God-toward-man is far more significant than that of man-toward-God. It is what God does in the sacrament that gives it vitality and validity—not what we do. And this point of view must undergird every explanation of the sacrament. It is not an "extra" added to The Service now and then for special occasions. You will want to set this sacramental character of worship before pupils, and yet it too must be limited because it has such far-reaching implications and you need to budget your time.

This would be the point at which you could bear heavily on the sacramental character of our church. We commune at the *Lord's* table, and at *his* invitation (we don't invite him to be present or even invoke his presence as we do at mealtime; he invites us). It's what he gives through the sacrament that counts; not how impressive it may be or the frame of mind we're in. Help pupils feel how our worship assumes the presence of God throughout—the Communion liturgy especially. The purpose of this liturgy is not to manufacture the right mood, but to respond to his loving presence.

You might sharpen this by indicating certain things that we discount: the impressiveness of the Communion Service; the personality of the minister; the touches of "soft music" and "solemn faces." If the Communion Service is regarded as impressive, it's because it notes God's presence and voices our praise.

Your pupils may like to sit together the next time your church has a Communion Service. Perhaps the pastor would meet with the group briefly following the service to answer any questions they might have regarding the Communion practices in your church.

3. Examine the Communion liturgy.

Pupils may wonder about the use of the Lord's Prayer by the minister here. Indicate that this is the one place where this occurs, and that the minister performs a priestly role in praying it on behalf of the whole congregation.

The seasonal prefaces (SBH pp. 9–10) may be scanned for their special emphases, the tone of the sacrament during a particular season of the church year.

Various methods of administering Communion need not be discussed here, as the Communion Service does not include any direction about method. However, the words connected with the administration of bread and wine might be noted as reminders to communicants of the presence of Christ.

Some attention may also be given the Post-Communion. Its brevity might be noted; also its double focus of thankfulness and dedication. Following the pupil's book, you might liken a person's leaving church before the Communion Service is completed to a bad-mannered guest rushing away from his host's dinner table with a flying, "Thank you."

4. Explore the Bible passages.

Help the pupils see that the tag lines given with the passages tip off their location in the Communion liturgy. Luke 24:28–35 might be studied for its relevance to communing (Jesus making himself known through the breaking of bread), and the Revelation passage for its emphasis on the note on which worship concludes.

Pencils may be needed for harmonizing the four accounts of the Words of Institution. According to the best authorities, Paul's account in 1 Corinthians 11:23–26 is probably the first written record of the Lord's Supper and antedates the Gospels. Pupils may note how heavily the Words of Institution leans on this Epistle record.

5. Discuss questions related to participating in Communion.

Raise a question about the practice of judging a person's active membership in his congregation by the number of times he communes in a year. Should the standard be at least once a year? If this forces a high spiritual moment to become a yardstick, does it tend to ask people to commune for poor reasons? What better yardstick could be found?

Shouldn't Christians commune because they want to, rather than because they feel that they have to just to keep their name on the role of active members?

Ask pupils for their opinions about the qualifications a person should have for communing. List the following qualifications on the board. Ask for pupils' reactions. (*a*) Membership in the congregation. (*b*) Good reputation. (*c*) Nice appearance. (*d*) Feeling of being worthy, holding head high. (*e*) Sense of sin. (*f*) Confession. (*g*) Fasting. (*h*) Feeling of need of forgiveness. (*i*) Wanting to be close to God.

Question Six presents an uneven group of qualifications. Possibly (*a*), (*e*), (*f*), (*h*), and (*i*) would be the best answers. (*g*) might be answered in terms of the Catechism's emphasis on a believing heart, rather than an external discipline. (*c*) is often considered important by church members, but is a misunderstanding of Communion: "I don't have nice clothes to wear so I can't possibly commune." (*d*) is a real problem. When a man thinks he is worthy, he is forgetting his sins and is in need of forgiveness.

Discuss what worshipers should do while others commune. Suggest certain devotional practices: the reading of parts of the service book, including appropriate hymns and prayers, or getting our thoughts ironed out through quiet meditation.

6. Review the course.

Use materials from the additional session to pull the course together. Omit this step if you plan to use the session by itself next week.

---

an additional session for unit G (optional)
SCOPE OF THE SESSION

This session has a threefold purpose: to help the pupil (1) to gather up loose threads of the whole term; (2) to review quickly the peaks in both terms; (3) to glimpse the scope of next year's course. Your progress to date will determine the time needed for the first two purposes. In your own preparation reread the unit introductions for this term, largely to see what unfinished business lies before you. Also scan quickly the first term in the pupil's book for points you may wish to include in a quick review.

MATERIALS NEEDED

Pupil's book. Other materials depending on the unfinished work.

AN OVERVIEW OF THE SESSION

1. Review the course briefly.

2. Use review tests.

3. Give a brief preview of next year's course.

172

SESSION PLAN IN GREATER DETAIL

1. Review the course briefly.

Using the pupil's book as a guide, attempt a quick review of the course including areas of study and projects undertaken.

Relate the theme of God, the Father, whom we confess in the First Article of the Creed to our communication with him in prayer and worship. You might ask pupils which studies they enjoyed most, what chapters in their books gave them new insights, other questions they would like to discuss.

2. Use review tests.

You can use a quickie quiz with scrambled words. Put these words on the board and ask pupils to straighten out the printer's mistakes and explain the words as best they can. They are all terms associated with the worship of the church. Give them an example such as: If SPELGO were one of the words, you would first unscramble it as "Gospel," then explain it as "the Bible lesson taken from the life and works of Jesus."

NOITRIT	(Introit—"entrance" to The Service; verses from Psalms that set the tone or mood for the day's worship.)
SNUGA IDE	(Agnus Dei—"Lamb of God"; the chant used in the Communion liturgy.)
SPETLIE	(Epistle—Bible lesson taken from an epistle, or letter.)
CNUSSAT	(Sanctus—"Holy"; chant of praise in the Communion liturgy.)
ARGILO TRIAP	(Gloria Patri—"Glory to the Father"; chant sung after Psalm verses to give a Christian ending to Old Testament verses.)
VEDO	(Dove—symbol of the Holy Spirit.)
TRAAL	(Altar—box-shaped furnishing, central in Lutheran churches because of links with Lord's Supper.)
VENA	(Nave—name for seating space in churches.)
CLOTELC	(Collect—brief prayer that either collects thoughts of pray-ers or thoughts of the day in prayer form.)
BRAVE	(Verba—"Words of Institution"; the words Jesus used in instituting the Lord's Supper.)

You could also pass out the pupils' answer papers to the check test ("What Do You Think About God?") in Unit C. Ask them if their ideas changed over the weeks of the course.

Whether you use one or both of these testing devices, allow time for pupils to think over the questions. Discuss their answers with them.

If you decide to use the check test from Unit C again, it would be well to consider mimeographing the test. Then pupils could give their present answers without seeing the answers they gave earlier.

3. Give a brief preview of next year's course.

Help the pupils see how this course leads to the next one. Use the "I believe . . . I respond" pattern to show them the structure of the catechetical years of study.

	I Believe . . .	I Respond . . .
Seventh Grade	in God the Father.	in prayer and worship (Lord's Prayer and The Service).
Eighth Grade	in God the Son.	in Christian living (Ten Commandments).
Ninth Grade	in God the Holy Spirit.	in sacraments (Baptism and Lord's Supper) and the church.

Help pupils feel that their double study this year will provide a base for next year. In the Sunday church school they have been studying the broad facts of Christ's life; in this course they have studied God the Father's work as Creator, Provider, Protector. They should now be ready to probe the saving work of redemption—God in Christ coming to save all men who believe in him—the very heart of the Christian gospel.

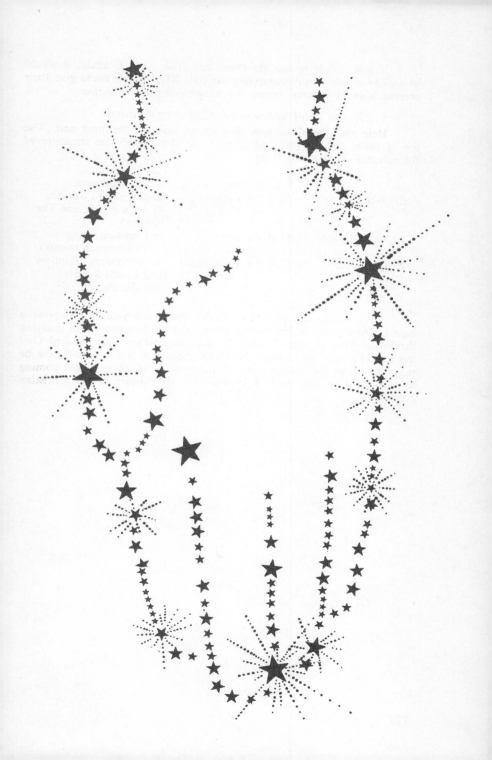